Choral Music
for
Children

Choral Music for Children

An Annotated List

MUSIC EDUCATORS NATIONAL CONFERENCE

Copyright ©1990
Music Educators National Conference
1902 Association Drive, Reston, Virginia 22091
All rights reserved.
Printed in the United States of America
ISBN 0-940796-80-5

Participation in music performance ranks among those activities that define a good life in society.... Some things must be worth doing for their own sake; musical excellence is then the only proper justification for learning to do them.
—Francis Sparshott, in *The New Grove Dictionary of Music and Musicians*

Contents

Contributors

Doreen Rao, editor, earned a bachelor of science in music education from the University of Illinois and received her master of music and Ph.D. in music education from Northwestern University. She is currently director of the Choral Music Experience Institute for Choral Teacher Education and director of choral programs and professor of music at the University of Toronto. Before her appointment at the University of Toronto, she held the dual position of assistant conductor of the Chicago Symphony Chorus and music director and conductor of the Glen Ellyn Children's Chorus.

Linda Beaupre majored in music education, with concentrations in piano and voice, at the State University of New York in Potsdam. She received her master of music degree in vocal performance from the University of Western Ontario. She sings with the Elmer Iseler Singers and the Toronto Mendelssohn Choir. She is the conductor of the Amadeus Children's Chorus in Scarborough, Ontario.

Nancy Boone received degrees in music education from Tennessee Wesleyan College, the University of Tennessee, and the University of Illinois, where she earned an Ed.D. in music education. Boone is a member of MENC and assistant professor of music at Middle Tennessee State University in Murfreesboro, Tennessee, where for the past ten years she has taught music education methods and K–6 at the University Laboratory School.

Mary Goetze earned a bachelor of music degree from Oberlin College in Ohio, a master of music education degree from Indiana University, and a Ph.D. in music education from the University of Colorado School of Music. Noted for her expertise in the development of the child's singing voice, she is director of the University Children's Chorus, a faculty member in the Music Education Department at Indiana University School of Music, and a member of MENC.

Joan Gregoryk studied at the College of St. Catherine, St. Paul, Minnesota, where she earned a bachelor of arts degree in music education. She was awarded a master of arts degree in music education from the University of Maryland. She teaches music at Chevy Chase Elementary School in Chevy Chase, Maryland. During the past twelve years she has prepared her children's chorus for performances and recordings with the National Symphony Orchestra. Gregoryk is a member of MENC who teaches courses on children's vocal development and the directs the children's choirs at Westminster Choir College in Princeton, New Jersey, and at Hamline University in St. Paul, Minnesota.

Preface

In 1977, *Music for Children's Choir: A Selective and Graded Listing* was published by the Music Educators National Conference and edited and compiled with the help of the American Choral Directors Association. When the MENC Publications Planning Committee determined that an updated version should be written and asked me to chair the new publication project, I suggested that the ACDA National Committee on Children's Choirs participate in this work. A committee of experts in the field of children's choirs, representing ACDA and MENC, was appointed and began its task in 1988.

The five-member committee represents a dedicated and inspired group of United States and Canadian teachers who direct children's choirs in school, university, and community settings. Each member of the committee proposed selected listings and annotated them for consideration and editing. I am indebted to the members of this committee, who devoted considerable time and talent to the completion of this publication project, and I thank them for their contributions to *Choral Music for Children: An Annotated List.*

DOREEN RAO

Introduction

During the past two years, members of the American Choral Directors Association National Committee on Children's Choirs have worked in close cooperation with the Music Educators National Conference in the preparation of *Choral Music for Children: An Annotated List*. This project was undertaken to provide teacher/conductors with a sourcebook on choral repertoire suitable for the teaching and learning of vocal music in school and community music programs.

The selections included in this text are limited to the unchanged, treble voice. The repertoire was selected and annotated on the basis of its artistic merit and pedagogical value. The committee of experts advising this publication recommended a wide variety of musical styles: from folk and traditional musics, to composed works of the Renaissance and Baroque, to Contemporary music. It is hoped that this broad range of repertoire will meet the artistic and pedagogical needs of both nonselect classroom choirs as well as select auditioned choirs.

Choral Music for Children was compiled and annotated as a resource to guide teachers in their choice of composed and arranged works now available in published form. In it, some three hundred choral works are discussed, each having been field-tested by a group of experts who successfully taught and performed these works in a variety of school and community settings. The selected annotations are arranged alphabetically by composer's last name. This form of presentation encourages us to appreciate musical works contextually, as works of art, crafted by a particular composer at a particular time in history.

The titles listed reflect the published and catalogued titles. Where two languages are involved, the translation is indicated in parentheses following the published title—for example: "Schubert, Franz; Fischerweise (Fisherman's Song)." Where titles are derived from extended works or from a grouping of related works, the source of the excerpt is indicated in parentheses following the title—for example: "Bach, Johann Sebastian; Domine Deus (from the Mass in G Major)."

Publishers are named in each entry and publisher octavo numbers are given in the majority of entries. Published choral music is distributed by local music dealers throughout the country, and the titles included in this annotated list are in print as this book goes to press. Music educators should feel comfortable about familiarizing local dealers with their printed music needs; the industry is anxious to serve music education by providing quality choral music suitable for children's choirs. Teacher and music administrators must be direct about their musical and pedagogical needs, discouraging the proliferation of "junk" music or "amusement" music and purchasing only the kind of music that fits educationally into a well-balanced choral program. The music purchased by schools must provide an opportunity for music education, a concept altogether different from "entertainment."

The authors have sought to include a wide range of styles and periods of choral music. The music of Johann Sebastian Bach forms a rather substantive beginning to the book; the authors feel that the interaction between Baroque harmony and counterpoint makes the music of Bach particularly valuable for young choirs. There is a substantial body of folk-song arrangements, including a good number of American and Canadian titles. The annotations selected to represent contemporary choral music for young choirs reflect a cross section of well-known composers and newly discovered talent.

The annotated list includes choral music in many different languages: most of the non-English folk-song arrangements include both the original language and an optional English text for singing. Whenever possible, teachers should consider using the original language rather than the translation. It is often possible to find a colleague or friend who will coach an unfamiliar language, and children respond eagerly to singing in other languages.

The annotations were written to provide insight into the characteristic qualities, forms, and styles of the selected entries. Each contributor annotated her project contributions from a musical and pedagogical perspective, relying on many years of teaching experience with young children. The pedagogical value of each entry was analyzed and, in some cases, teaching suggestions are offered.

The annotations are cross-referenced by composer or arranger (Index One); by title (Index Two); by voicing (Index Three); and by level of difficulty (Index Four). The index by composer can assist teachers in studying the choral works of a particular composer or in developing a choral program around a favorite composer or period. The title index is beneficial for developing a specialized choral program around a theme or special occasion. With regard to voicing, the index includes works listed under the headings unison, two-part treble, three-part treble, and four-part treble. This index will be valuable for music educators who work with very young choirs and who want to choose only unison and two-part music for their students.

The fourth index lists the composer and title by level of difficulty. There are four broad categories used for this index, including music for beginning, intermediate, and advanced choirs. The fourth category is a special listing of music for very young choirs (K–3). Teachers may interpret these categories differently according to their students' level of experience and expertise, the years of choral tradition established in the school or community program, and the teacher's own level of vocal/choral expertise. For example, fifth and sixth graders who have been taught to use their singing voice and who are vocally secure may find some two-part music included in the intermediate category to be "easy." Similarly, third graders who have not yet found the singing voice (or head voice mechanism) may find a unison song referenced in the beginning category to be "difficult."

The beginning category lists works that the committee felt were immediately accessible (mostly unison works, but also some two-part works with a limited range). The intermediate category lists works that were assessed as unison, two-part, and three-part works with a wider range and more technical challenge. The advanced category lists works that were rated as musically challenging but moderately difficult in two or more parts. On the subject of what is "easy" and what is "difficult," there is at least one important factor to consider: a child who has developed the singing voice, or head voice, can successfully perform music that the child still vocalizing in the speaking voice, or chest voice, cannot. The first task of the teacher teaching classroom singing or children's choirs is to teach the child how to find and use the singing voice. Whether or not a child can successfully perform a particular work at any level of difficulty depends on whether the child has been taught to use the voice for singing.

The listing of music for very young choirs was prepared for teachers working with children ages 5–7. Like all elementary-age children, these children can maintain a beautiful head tone, with good intonation, open vowels, and a lovely legato line. However, the technical ability to sing this way cannot be taken for granted. More than in any other age group, these skills must be taught through the repertoire selected. In this category there is very little that is bouncy or requires a forte dynamic level, as children will lose their singing sound (head tone) very quickly under those musical circumstances. The upper range in this category is generally limited to $E\flat_5$ or E_5, the lower range to C_4. (All notes and ranges in this book are give in the notation adopted by the U.S.A. Standards Association: C_4 is middle C.) Many of the youngest children do not sing well outside that range.

Teacher/conductors will want to choose choral music for their programs that includes a variety of composers, titles, styles, and textures that are thoughtfully balanced to include easily accessible music along with more challenging repertoire. Nevertheless, the cross-references in the four indexes of this publication should make the job of selecting appropriate choral music for special occasions a little easier.

The Children's Choir and Music Education

Choral singing is a form of musical experience that is valuable for all children. In contemporary music education, many scholars and practitioners agree that performing music is the major means for musical experience. Despite the prevalence of general music, a large number of music teachers continue to see themselves as choral music educators, Orff specialists, Kodály educators, and so on. The focus for many of the programs of these teachers continues to be music education through music performance and the concomitant achievement of recognized standards of musical excellence. Indeed, according to the Crane Symposium, music education conceived as music performance is still the biggest single preoccupation of the profession.

Public school music education began with choral singing over 150 years ago. Lowell Mason convinced the Boston School Board that the ability to perform music with the singing voice was important for all children, rather than just a talented few. During the 1967 MENC Tanglewood Symposium, America's most distinguished composers, conductors, and music educators agreed that the opportunity to perform music should be made available to all children at every stage of schooling. Numerous reports concerning music education assert that it is the obligation of education to provide opportunities for all persons to participate in the performing arts. These traditional democratic ideals suggest that all students should have the opportunity to be challenged and motivated through active participation in music performance.

The recent renaissance of singing in elementary school music programs has provided impetus for the development of children's choirs in school districts throughout the country. Choral singing opportunities are increasing in North America wherever there is an interest in music and the music education of children. There is little doubt that classroom singing and choral performance is reclaiming its rightful place in school music programs as an important component of the school curriculum.

The growing trend in children's choirs is supported by an impressive amount of music education research on the child voice and a growing body of research on the children's choir. The *Music Educators Journal* and the *Choral Journal* regularly devote space to this specialized area of music education. Special issues that dealt with the children's choir include the December 1988 *Music Educators Journal* and the March 1989 *Choral Journal*. Research journals, including the *The Bulletin of the Council for Research in Music Education* and the *Journal of Research in Music Education,* reflect a substantial amount of graduate and postgraduate research on the specialized skills associated with classroom singing and children's choirs.

Teachers, administrators, and parents often associate the children's choir with the ideal of "excellence." Choral singing opportunities for children seem to rank among those things that define a good life. In fact, performing experiences can be enjoyed and esteemed for their own sake. Surely the ideals of choral music performance are central to the democratic ideal—an ideal that challenges and motivates children to learn and improve. Where our aim is to enable children to participate in music performance and enjoy choral singing for its own sake, excellence is a strong justification.

The need to encourage choral singing in school music programs where all children can benefit from the study and performance of vocal music is an important objective for the music education profession. The essence of music performance is the music itself. Each new musical work is an opportunity for children to experience and express the great ideas of choral art. In music performance, instruction starts with particular works of music, rather than concepts about music. Through choral singing, children can develop the vocal and musicianship skills associated with producing and understanding the melody, rhythm, harmony, timbre, dynamics, and text of a variety of musical forms and styles.

Choral Repertoire for Music Instruction

While the choral repertoire should provide a balanced offering of styles and levels of complexity, it should always challenge and motivate musical learning. Teachers can transform the challenges of learning great choral music into an opportunity for musical discovery, musical problem solving, and skill development. The choral repertoire provides the foundation for musical instruction. When the quality of repertoire is excellent, the teaching potential is unlimited. The musical ideas found in great choral music have unusual pedagogical value. The study and performance of great choral literature will yield good returns for the time invested in its study.

With regard to choral music in music education, the following conditions will contribute toward a successful choral program:

- The music should be excellent. Only the best-quality choral repertoire should be considered for inclusion in the school music program. Unison, two-part, and three-part songs should be organized in a carefully planned choral curriculum.
- The music itself should be the central focus and purpose of instruction. The repertoire should include a balanced offering from simple and accessible music to more complex and challenging examples in a wide variety of styles and periods. This varied repertoire should include American folk music (including arranged traditional forms, spirituals, and gospel songs), choral classics, such as the works of Bach, Handel,

Schubert, and Brahms; and music by contemporary composers such as Britten, Bartók, and Kodály. It should also include American contemporary music, such as that of Copland, Pinkham, Rorem, and Nelson; jazz classics representing North American culture; and commissioned works for children's choirs.

- The teaching/directing should be sequenced and musical. Music education through choral performance is achieved in rehearsals that stress the development of musicianship—the musical skill and understanding associated with artistic performance. Based on the artistic model for performance-based music instruction, classroom and choir rehearsals should provide students with opportunities to produce music through regular singing experiences, to practice musicianship skills associated with vocal production and musical understanding, and to perform the music artistically, with skill and understanding. Teaching music through performance requires the ability to use nonverbal methods of instruction, including vocal modeling, conducting, solfège, and movement techniques.

- The outcomes of performance-based music education should include the enjoyment of music for its own sake. Music education through choral performance is a way of teaching children how to make music and how to understand music; a way of delving deeply into the musical elements, form, and style expressed in the particular works being studied; a way of teaching vocal skills, music reading skills and musical knowledge; and a way of enjoying music for its own sake.

Choral repertoire and musical performance go hand in hand in music education. In this context, the study and performance of choral music is a way of educating children musically through skillful participation in the making of music. As music educators learn to trust the traditional ideals of excellence, they will again view music performance as something worth doing for its own sake. Musical performance challenges children to improve—to transcend the ordinary in favor of something superior. These goals are realized through musical encounters with choral repertoire that inspires and motivates children to learn.

6

Annotations

Composer: Bach, Johann Sebastian
Title: Bist Du Bei Mir
Publisher: Gordon V. Thompson Music G-183
Voicing: Unison, piano accompaniment
Style: Baroque
Language: German/English
Notes: The stirring melody from the *Notebook for Anna Magdalena Bach* has been harmonized by S. Calvert in this arrangement. Even though the topic of the text is serious and intensely religious, the beautiful melody is immediately appealing to children.
Pedagogical value: The key and tessitura are perfect for young voices, and singing the long, arching phrases will contribute to improved vocal control.
Level of difficulty: Intermediate

Composer: Bach, Johann Sebastian
Title: Domine Deus (from the Mass in G major)
Publisher: Boosey & Hawkes OC2B6552
Voicing: Two parts, piano accompaniment, violins optional
Style: Baroque
Language: Latin
Notes: This duet forms the central section of the "Gloria" of Bach's Mass in G major and demonstrates an ideal interaction of harmony and counterpoint. As one of Bach's four small ("Lutheran") masses, some scholars suggest that this mass was among Bach's preliminary studies for the B minor Mass. The duet offers a musical challenge and can be studied and performed successfully by children's choirs who rehearse on a regular basis.
Pedagogical value: The study of this masterpiece offers young choirs the opportunity to develop the vocal and musicianship skills necessary to sing the music of Bach successfully. These skills include an understanding of the musical elements of pitch and rhythm, a grasp of the form, and an ability to perform in an appropriate style. The vocal skills required include those associated with posture, breath management, and the principles of vocal diction.
Level of difficulty: Advanced

Composer: Bach, Johann Sebastian
Title: Flocks in Pastures Green Abiding
Publisher: Oxford #OCS 1631
Voicing: Unison, piano or orchestra accompaniment
Style: Baroque
Language: German/English
Notes: This familiar aria, with its gently lyrical interludes, is accessible to young choirs. Shaping the long phrases may challenge some singers, but the musical and vocal benefits are insured.
Pedagogical value: This piece is a nice way to introduce children to the Baroque style. Every attempt should be made to perform it with period instruments rather than with the piano.
Level of difficulty: Intermediate

Composer: Bach, Johann Sebastian
Title: "Gloria! the World Rejoices" (Gloria Sei Dir Gesungen)
Publisher: Gordon V. Thompson Music G-195
Voicing: Unison, piano accompaniment
Style: Baroque
Language: German/English
Notes: Attributed to Philip Nicolai (1556–1608), the familiar melody from Cantata No. 140 is harmonized by J. S. Bach. The D major melody moves in a maestoso tempo, tastefully realized for keyboard accompaniment by Voltr Ivonoffski. The easy to sing unison melody outlines the traditional chordal progression I, IV, V, I.
Pedagogical value: Students can explore both the harmonic and melodic qualities of this choral classic by practicing the D major scale, by singing the chordal outlines, and by solfegging the main melodic patterns inherent in this familiar tune.
Level of difficulty: Beginning; for very young choirs

Composer: Bach, Johann Sebastian; arr. Doreen Rao
Title: How Brightly Shines the Morning Star (chorale melody, Cantata No. 1)
Publisher: Boosey & Hawkes #OCUB6418
Voicing: Unison, piano accompaniment
Style: Baroque
Language: German/English
Notes: The idea that young choirs can enjoy singing Bach masterpieces serves as the guiding principle of this edition. Using a well-known chorale melody harmonized by Bach in Cantata No. 1, the arranger extracts the chorale melody to be sung in unison by the children's choir. The four-part harmonization is used as keyboard accompaniment. Once the young singers have mastered the melody, one can add the alto voice part from the four-part harmonization. Another performance option involves the addition of an SATB choir for festival performances or for joint concerts with mixed chorus.
Pedagogical value: The singing of a Bach chorale melody can serve as an early introduction to the music of J. S. Bach. Students can study and perform this famous melody in many settings by Bach, including the treble-voice duet from Bach's Cantata No. 37. The range of this melody is wide and serves to inspire the development of supported head tone. The descending melody lines are ideally suited to bring the singing voice (or head voice mechanism) down into the lower range.
Level of difficulty: Beginning

Composer: Bach, Johann Sebastian
Title: I Will Praise the Lord (duet from Cantata No. 37)
Publisher: Boosey & Hawkes #OC2B6413
Voicing: Two parts, piano accompaniment
Style: Baroque
Language: German/English

Notes: This treble-voice duet from Cantata No. 37 is based on the famous melody, "How Brightly Shines the Morning Star"—a melody that Bach used in Cantatas 1, 49, 61, and 172. This edition is arranged for children's choirs in a practice similar to that of Bach's original performances with the St. Thomas's Church boy's choir in Leipzig. The melismatic voice parts are based on the chorale melody and can be easily traced throughout the duet. The lilting compound meter and dancelike tempo offer an intermediate or advanced children's choir the opportunity to perform the music of Bach in its original form.

Pedagogical value: Ideally, singers should approach this duet by learning the related unison chorale melody, "How Brightly Shines the Morning Star," from Cantata No. 1. As the singers perform the melody of this chorale, they discover its two-part form, which relates directly to the duet material. The study and performance of this duet offers young students the opportunity to develop the singing and musicianship skills required for singing long, melismatic lines in compound meter.

Level of difficulty: Advanced

Composer: Bach, Johann Sebastian
Title: Laughing and Shouting for Joy (duet from Cantata No. 15)
Publisher: Boosey & Hawkes #OC2B6454
Voicing: Two parts, piano accompaniment
Style: Baroque
Language: German/English
Notes: Bach's treble-voice duet is perfectly suited for the children's choir. The easy contrapuntal subjects remain distinct and fun to sing. The children enjoy differentiating between the "laughing and shouting" subject, set in lighthearted arpeggios, and the "crying and sighing" countersubject, set in sustained, descending chromatics. The simple AB da capo form shapes this short and accessible duet. The performance can be enhanced with the unison violin material included in the edition.
Pedagogical value: The study and performance of Bach duets offers an opportunity for young choirs to develop an understanding of form, word painting, harmony, and texture. The editor's notes include an analysis of the duet and teaching suggestions for the study and performance of Bach.
Level of difficulty: Intermediate

Composer: Bach, Johann Sebastian
Title: Lord, See the Good Works of My Heart (duet from Cantata No. 9)
Publisher: Boosey & Hawkes #OC2B6362
Voicing: Two parts, piano accompaniment
Style: Baroque
Language: German/English
Notes: This duet does not involve a chorale melody. The vocal parts are imitative and fun to sing. Bach scored the duet for treble voices in canon, flute and oboe d'amore in canon, and continuo with organ. The A section is developed in A major with simple even rhythms in duple meter. The B section is built on a syncopated rhythmic motive in the dominant. The voice parts remain independent and always dancelike.
Pedagogical value: The whole choir can begin the study and performance of this piece by singing the first theme as it appears in the upper treble and lower treble voice parts. The young choir can sing, clap, and chant the material: first without text and then with text (working from rhythm to pitch). Doing this, young choirs develop the musicianship skills necessary to count and sing in tune.
Level of difficulty: Advanced

Composer: Bach, Johann Sebastian
Title: Rejoice, O My Spirit (aria from Cantata No. 15)
Publisher: G. Schirmer
Voicing: Unison, piano accompaniment
Style: Baroque
Language: English
Notes: As was the case for many cantata arias, original performance practice of this piece called for small groups of treble voices rather than solo singers. The lilting compound meter is melodically melismatic but not difficult to sing as a unison choir.
Pedagogical value: Through the study and performance of the Bach aria sung by unison choir, young students experience the genius of Bach. Through the contrasting musical elements of high and low, long and short, bright and dark, Bach conveys the meaning of good versus evil.
Level of difficulty: Beginning; for very young choirs

Composer: Bach, Johann Sebastian
Title: Wir eilen mit schwachen, doch emsigen Schritten (We Hasten with Faltering Footsteps: duet from Cantata No. 78)
Publisher: E. C. Schirmer #2506
Voicing: Two parts, piano accompaniment
Style: Baroque
Language: German/English
Notes: This is a classic of children's choral literature, cherished by singers and conductors alike. The beautiful phrases and imitative counterpoint are a superb way for developing singers to come to know Bach and make a fine piece on which to "cut their musical teeth."
Pedagogical value: Its long, melismatic lines, which paint the word "hurry" in forward-driving rhythms and ascending lines, can teach young singers much about music of this period while helping the choristers develop vocal skills. Less experienced choirs sometimes attempt only the first section of the *da capo* form.
Level of difficulty: Advanced

Composer: Bacon, Ernst
Title: Buttermilk Hill
Publisher: Boosey & Hawkes #5944
Voicing: Two parts; piano or organ accompaniment with bells, small drum, or tambourine (optional violin, flute, or recorder)
Style: English folk
Language: English
Notes: This arrangement achieves a stark simplicity by the continuous use of B and F♯ in the accompaniment. The simple and intensely expressive accompaniment enhances the lamenting text and melody.
Pedagogical value: Children benefit from learning to sing vertical intervals of fifths and fourths, in addition to the traditional thirds, against the melody. The basic rhythm patterns in the instrumental parts are quite playable by children.
Level of difficulty: Intermediate

Composer: Bartók, Béla
Title: Breadbaking
Publisher: Boosey & Hawkes #1669
Voicing: Two parts, unaccompanied (optional orchestral accompaniment)
Style: Contemporary
Language: English
Notes: The rhythmic motion, imitation, and lively pace make this piece challenging and yet fun for young singers. Each short section of text is set apart by a tempo change; these sections make logical units for teaching.
Pedagogical value: This is an effective piece for acquainting singers with the sound of the Lydian mode in a contemporary style and for developing their part singing skills. The style and tempo require clean, staccato articulation of text.
Level of difficulty: Advanced

Composer: Bartók, Béla
Title: Don't Leave Me
Publisher: Boosey & Hawkes #1668
Voicing: Two parts, unaccompanied (optional orchestral accompaniment)
Style: Contemporary
Language: English
Notes: This piece is a stark contrast to "Breadbaking"—both in its expressive style and in the content of the text, although it also has Lydian passages and is imitative. "Don't Leave Me" has long, flowing phrases that require a quiet yet intense delivery of the poignant text.
Pedagogical value: The dynamics range from intense and soft to full-voice singing. Students learn to sing vertical and horizontal intervals in the Lydian mode and become acquainted with the mode's effect.
Level of difficulty: Intermediate

Composer: Baynon, Arthur
Title: Mrs. Jenny Wren
Publisher: Boosey & Hawkes OCUB6117
Voicing: Unison, piano accompaniment
Style: Contemporary
Language: English
Notes: The text of this piece was written by Rodney Bennett. There are two strophic verses and a through-composed piano accompaniment. The piece is in E♭ major, in $\frac{4}{4}$ time, with a range from E♭$_4$ to E♭$_5$.
Pedagogical value: This is a very short, easy, and charming composition. Its steady eighth and quarter notes might require discussing the creation of sustained sounds through open vowels to achieve a legato line. In the first verse, the singer tells Mrs. Jenny Wren that she has never heard such a big voice for such a tiny bird; in the second verse, the singer says that she would never dare sing as loudly but would sing very softly (sung piano)—or the listeners would hurry away with a finger in each ear.
Level of difficulty: Beginning; for very young choirs

Composer: Beethoven, Ludwig van
Title: Abbé Stadler
Publisher: Boosey & Hawkes OC3B6368
Voicing: Three-part canon, unaccompanied
Style: Classical
Language: Latin/German
Notes: This three-voice canon sounds serious, but the text is not—it is a teasing threat to Beethoven's local priest.
Pedagogical value: Children will enjoy meeting Beethoven's verbal and musical humor; the vocal line containing the devilish threat is set to a sequence of suspensions that create horrendous momentary dissonances against the other voices.
Level of difficulty: Intermediate

Composer: Berger, Jean
Title: A Child's Book of Beasts, Sets I and II
Publisher: J. Fischer & Brother. Set I: FEC9562; Set II: FEC 9796
Voicing: Two parts, piano accompaniment
Style: Contemporary
Language: English
Notes: These two sets comprise a total of twelve pieces: Set one includes "The Yak," "The Polar Bear," "The Dromedary," "The Hippopotamus," "The Rhinoceros," and "The Frog"; set two has "The Lion—The Tiger," "The Dodo," "The Whale," "The Big Baboon," "The Elephant," and "The Marozet." The texts by Hilaire Belloc are very silly, and their jocularity is reflected in the music. The textures range from unison to imitative counterpoint and parallel thirds.
Pedagogical value: Children enjoy singing these and grow musically in the process of mastering the melodic lines, which range from lyrical and flowing to angular and disjunct.
Level of difficulty: Intermediate

Composer: Berger, Jean
Title: Fin, Feather and Fur
Publisher: Shawnee Press B-379
Voicing: Three parts, piano accompaniment
Style: Contemporary
Language: English
Notes: This is a set of three poem settings: "Morning at the Beach" by John Farrar, "The Vulture" by Hilaire Belloc, "The Caterpillar" by Christina Rossetti. The texts are fun—some are even inane—and entirely appropriate for children; the music is quite accessible.
Pedagogical value: The part-writing in these songs provides an introduction to singing in parallel thirds, and the rhythm in "Caterpillar" demands careful articulation of words in a quick $\frac{6}{8}$.
Level of difficulty: Intermediate

Composer: Berkowitz, Sol
Title: Don't Ask Me!
Publisher: Lawson-Gould #52056
Voicing: Two parts, piano accompaniment
Style: Contemporary
Language: English
Notes: The fantastical text of this piece has immediate appeal to young singers and motivates them to master the wide intervals of the melody. This accessible contemporary piece has many altered tones in the accompaniment and melody. The ranges of the two parts are rather low for head-voice singing (C_4 to C_5 and A_3 to F_4).
Pedagogical value: The octave and seventh leaps in the melody line will contribute to children's vocal skills and mastery of wide intervals. The second voice moves by half and whole steps and may be especially appropriate for singers of limited ability or boys whose voices are changing.
Level of difficulty: Intermediate

Composer: Berkowitz, Sol
Title: I Had a Little Pup
Publisher: Lawson-Gould 52057
Voicing: Two parts, piano accompaniment
Style: Contemporary
Language: English
Notes: This is a charming novelty piece with chromatic tones that yield phrases in Lydian and Mixolydian. The text is traditional and whimsical: each verse is set one half step higher than the previous one.
Pedagogical value: The voice leading accommodates beginning part-singers. Mastering the low alto line (G_3–G_4) without shouting facilitates vocal growth in young singers.
Level of difficulty: Intermediate

Composer: Bertaux, Betty
Title: An Apple with Its Seeds (from *Three Riddles*)
Publisher: Boosey & Hawkes #6190
Voicing: Four-part canon, unaccompanied
Style: Contemporary
Language: English
Notes: The text is splendid as poetry and as a riddle for children, and it is set very effectively in an unusual Dorian canon. The melody appears in two- and four-part canons culminating with slightly different melodic material in the work's coda.
Pedagogical value: This is a good way to introduce children to the sound of the Dorian mode and to reinforce their vocal independence. The other two riddles in this set (sold separately) are equally charming but much more challenging.
Level of difficulty: Intermediate

Composer: Bertaux, Betty, arr.

Title: May Day Carol

Publisher: Boosey & Hawkes #6358

Voicing: Three parts, piano accompaniment

Style: American folk

Language: English

Notes: This is the perfect ending selection for a spring concert! The simple melody is accompanied by a delicate piano countermelody. In the repetition of the three verses, two descant parts are added, building to a grand ending.

Pedagogical value: The simple melody is ideal for even the youngest choirs. They will learn to shape phrases and economize breath in order to sustain the elongated last note of each verse. When combining choirs of various skill levels, the two descants can be assigned effectively to the more advanced singers.

Level of difficulty: Intermediate

Composer: Bertaux, Betty, arr.

Title: Pick a Bale of Cotton

Publisher: Boosey & Hawkes #6191

Voicing: Two parts, unaccompanied (optional piano accompaniment)

Style: American folk

Language: English

Notes: The splendid motion of this lively tune is maintained from the beginning of the arrangement until the brief coda. The simple melody is divided between the two voices, accompanied by simple countermelodies based on melodic motives, and finally treated in a quick canon. The work is a delight for choirs of all ages to sing.

Pedagogical value: This arrangement offers opportunities for rhythmic development: challenges such as syncopation and ties appear in the varied forms of the melodic motives used in the countermelody. This piece also contributes to part singing skills. The polyphony is musically satisfying and tonally accessible.

Level of difficulty: Intermediate

Composer: Bertaux, Betty, arr.
Title: S'vivon
Publisher: Boosey & Hawkes #6193
Voicing: Four parts, unaccompanied
Style: Hebrew folk (Hannukah song)
Language: Hebrew
Notes: Bertaux has used three countermelodies to accompany this cherished Hannukah song about a dreydl (small top). Each voice reflects the continuous motion of the melody and yet has its own character. The piece builds from unison to two, three, and finally four voices.
Pedagogical value: This arrangement offers many opportunities to teach musical concepts such as melodic sequence and imitation. A short slow section that occurs just before the quick-moving coda allows the teaching of another pair of techniques: the rhythm of one phrase is augmented and harmonized in parallel sixths.
Level of difficulty: Intermediate

Composer: Bertaux, Betty, arr.
Title: To Music
Publisher: Boosey & Hawkes OCTB6573
Voicing: Unison with descant and piano (optional strings)
Style: Contemporary
Language: English
Notes: This sixteenth-century German chorale melody was arranged for unison treble choir. While the melody has been used to set a number of texts, any of which may be substituted, the text used by this arranger presents another perspective in praise of music. The piano accompaniment is tasteful and supports the melody line without overwhelming the vocal material.
Pedagogical value: The well-known melody is offered in three verses: verses one and two are sung in unison, and verse three arranged polyphonically with melody and descant. The four-bar phrases are classically arched, rhythmically sustained, and sung in legato style. The text is expressive and inspirational. The piece is appropriate for concerts and festivals.
Level of difficulty: Beginning

Composer: Bertaux, Betty, arr.
Title: Who Killed Cock Robin
Publisher: Boosey & Hawkes #6240
Voicing: Three parts, piano accompaniment
Style: American folk
Language: English
Notes: This familiar and beautiful folk song is set sensitively with simple flowing vocal countermelodies and a gentle, arpeggiated piano accompaniment. A few nondiatonic tones add poignancy to the sorrowful message expressed in text and melody. Children relish the introspective mood of this piece—a relief from the lighter expressions of so much of the music they sing.
Pedagogical value: The delayed entrance of the accompaniment after the a cappella introduction requires careful attention to intonation. Young singers will be successful in singing these parts because the accompanying vocal lines are folklike in character and the entrances are well prepared.
Level of difficulty: Beginning

Composer: Biggs, John, arr.
Title: Il court, le furet
Publisher: Theodore Presser #312-40525
Voicing: Three parts, unaccompanied
Style: French folk
Language: French/English
Notes: The lively French melody, the quick articulation of the text about a ferret, and the skillful part writing commend this piece for consideration. The melody is passed around among the voices throughout the arrangement.
Pedagogical value: Vocal independence can be exercised in the piece through attention to some of the simple but effective devices used by the arranger. For example, two voices sometimes move in parallel octaves while the third voice sustains a pitch; at other times two voices accompany the melody with simple ostinato patterns.
Level of difficulty: Intermediate

Composer: Binkerd, Gordon
Title: The Christ Child (No. 1 from *Sung Under the Silver Umbrella*)
Publisher: Boosey & Hawkes #5987
Voicing: Two parts, piano or harp accompaniment
Style: Contemporary
Language: English
Notes: An exquisite melody is woven throughout this setting of a Christmas text by Gilbert K. Chesterton. The theme is contrasted with a haunting ritornello section, out of which the composer builds a dramatic climax.
Pedagogical value: Singing the wide melodic intervals found in this piece results in increased vocal control. Once singers are familiar with this melody, even its leap of descending major seventh becomes as logical, singable, and inevitable as leaps of fourths or fifths.
Level of difficulty: Advanced

Composer: Binkerd, Gordon
Title: An Evening Falls (No. 3 from *Sung Under the Silver Umbrella*)
Publisher: Boosey & Hawkcs #5987
Voicing: Unison, piano accompaniment
Style: Contemporary
Language: English
Notes: Above a transcription of a blues by Jimi Hendrix, Binkerd has added a lyrical melody. The style of the accompaniment, in contrast to the light quality of children's voices articulating the unusual text, makes this piece a favorite of choristers and audiences.
Pedagogical value: This is an effective piece for learning to shape and sustain phrases, for refining unison singing, and for introducing choirs to the blues style.
Level of difficulty: Intermediate

Composer: Binkerd, Gordon
Title: Song of Innocence (No. 2 from *Sung Under the Silver Umbrella*)
Publisher: Boosey & Hawkes #5987
Voicing: Three parts, unaccompanied
Style: Contemporary
Language: English
Notes: William Blake's symbolic text has a clear structure and lends itself well to a musical setting. This one is particularly challenging and beautiful.
Pedagogical value: The unmetered rhythm, the chromatic lines, and the staggered entrances offer a chance to advance all aspects of musical development.
Level of difficulty: Advanced

Composer: Bissell, Keith
Title: When I Set Out for Lyonesse
Publisher: Gordon V. Thompson Music G-233
Voicing: Two parts, piano accompaniment
Style: Contemporary
Language: English
Notes: Bissell has set this enchanting text by Thomas Hardy to music with great sensitivity. The flowing style and sudden shifts of tonality paint a beautiful setting for the mystery in the poem.
Pedagogical value: The voice parts, weaving from unison to two and three parts in a style that is more homophonic than contrapuntal, offer opportunities for range development and sensitive, expressive singing.
Level of difficulty: Advanced

Composer: Boyce, William; arr. Richard Proulx
Title: Alleluia Round
Publisher: GIA Publications G-2494
Voicing: Three-part canon (optional accompaniment for organ, flute, two horns or trombones, and bass)
Style: Classical
Language: Latin
Notes: This lovely round, which can be sung with or without the accompaniment, is arranged and extended by adding instrumental parts that double and embellish the melodic line.
Pedagogical value: This work can provide choristers with a nice introduction to melismatic singing and part singing.
Level of difficulty: Beginning; for very young choirs

Composer: Brahms, Johannes
Title: Die Meere (Op. 20, No. 3)
Publisher: National Music Publishers WHC-57
Voicing: Two parts, piano accompaniment
Style: Romantic
Language: German/English
Notes: The voices move primarily in parallel thirds and sixths throughout this strophic duet. The melody is flowing and restful above the unyielding motion of the piano.
Pedagogical value: The phrases, typical of Brahms, provide an experience in subtle shaping of phrases and the use of quiet dynamics.
Level of difficulty: Intermediate

Composer: Brahms, Johannes
Title: Die Schwestern (Op. 61, No. 1)
Publisher: Neil A. Kjos Ed. 6166
Voicing: Two parts, piano accompaniment
Style: Romantic
Language: German/English
Notes: The phrases of this duet are vocally demanding but beautifully arched. Linda Anderson has provided a very singable English text along with the German.
Pedagogical value: Choristers will benefit from meeting the demands of the wide range called for in this piece. Careful attention must be given to articulation in staccato passages, which are abruptly contrasted with the legato sections.
Level of difficulty: Intermediate

Composer: Brahms, Johannes
Title: Marienwuermchen
Publisher: Boosey & Hawkes #OCUB6521
Voicing: Unison, piano accompaniment
Style: Romantic
Language: German/English
Notes: This simple song is from a collection of folk songs set by Brahms. The story, similar to our "Ladybug, Ladybug" nursery rhyme, is told in three verses.
Pedagogical value: For a first acquaintance with German music, the long phrases will provide beginning singers with the experience of sustaining their voices and shaping melodic lines. The intervals center on pitches of the tonic and dominant chords.
Level of difficulty: Beginning; for very young choirs

Composer: Britten, Benjamin
Title: The New Year Carol (No. 5 from *Friday Afternoons,* Op. 7)
Publisher: Boosey & Hawkes #5615
Voicing: Unison, piano accompaniment
Style: Contemporary
Language: English
Notes: This is one of those utterly beautiful melodies that children and their audiences love. The three verses contain symbolism that no one has definitely explained. Each verse is followed by a chorus, which builds to a musical climax and then resolves quietly. Many other singable unison songs from Britten's *Friday Afternoons* collection are published separately; the entire collection should be a staple in every children's chorus library.
Pedagogical value: This song can be an effective means to teach choristers to control phrasing and allargando passages, but the best reason to teach it is for the chorister's musical enjoyment.
Level of difficulty: Beginning; for very young choirs

Composer: Britten, Benjamin
Title: Old Abram Brown (No. 12 from *Friday Afternoons,* Op. 7)
Publisher: Boosey & Hawkes #1787
Voicing: Four-part canon, piano accompaniment
Style: Contemporary
Language: English
Notes: Britten paints a rather grim musical picture of this old man in the sometimes harsh and dissonant accompaniment. While the melody is simple, its treatment in the context of the piece as a whole makes it sound more complex than it is. Many other singable unison songs from Britten's *Friday Afternoons* collection are published separately. The entire collection should be a staple in every children's chorus library.
Pedagogical value: Britten's music provides many opportunities for musical concept and skill development by using the melody in a two-part canon, a four-part canon, and in augmentation.
Level of difficulty: Beginning; for very young choirs

Composer: Britten, Benjamin
Title: Oliver Cromwell
Publisher: Boosey & Hawkes #5893
Voicing: Unison, piano accompaniment
Style: English folk
Language: English
Notes: This is an example of Britten's brilliant compositional technique: he perfectly complements the familiar $\frac{6}{8}$ folk song with a light, quick accompaniment. As always, his harmonization is inventive and refreshing.
Pedagogical value: Beginning singers can perform this artistically—in part because the vocal range promotes a light sound and the text is easy, fun, and quick-moving.
Level of difficulty: Beginning; for very young choirs

Composer: Britten, Benjamin, arr.
Title: The Sally Gardens
Publisher: Boosey & Hawkes #5448
Voicing: Unison, piano accompaniment
Style: Irish folk
Language: English
Notes: This is another of Britten's lovely folk song arrangements. To this slow, lyrical melody, he has introduced a repeated eighth-note patterns, played in thirds. The harmonic interest in the piano parts add an unusually expressive quality to this famous folk song.
Pedagogical value: Children respond to the tender sentiment expressed in the text and music. Sustaining the beautiful phrases will contribute to breath and pitch control.
Level of difficulty: Beginning; for very young choirs

Composer: Britten, Benjamin
Title: This Little Babe (from *A Ceremony of Carols,* Op. 28)
Publisher: Boosey & Hawkes #5138
Voicing: Three parts, harp or piano accompaniment
Style: Contemporary
Language: English
Notes: This is perhaps the best-known of the choruses from Britten's *A Ceremony of Carols,* and it is a favorite of young choirs. The texture begins with a unison statement of the melody, which in the subsequent verses expands to presentation in two- and three-part canons. A number of other choruses from *A Ceremony of Carols* are also published separately.
Pedagogical value: The fast tempo and motion of the sweeping melody will improve choristers' articulation skills. The work's greatest challenge and value to musical development come with maintaining a three-part canon with one beat between voices. The rhythm of the melody is presented in augmentation and briefly shifts to major in the coda.
Level of difficulty: Intermediate

Composer: Broughton, Marilyn
Title: My Caterpillar
Publisher: Gordon V. Thompson Music G-185
Voicing: Unison, piano accompaniment
Style: Contemporary
Language: English
Notes: The text of this piece was written by the composer. It is in B♭ major, in $\frac{6}{8}$, with a range from D_4 to $E\flat_5$.
Pedagogical value: This is a charming, moderately easy, through-composed account of a child making friends with a caterpillar. Choristers can practice the many slurred pairs of eighth notes within groups of three and the many dynamic contrasts in the work.
Level of difficulty: Beginning; for very young choirs

Composer: Broughton, Marilyn
Title: Nursery Rhyme Nonsense
Publisher: Gordon V. Thompson Music G-184
Voicing: Unison, piano accompaniment
Style: Contemporary
Language: English
Notes: The simplicity and humor of this simple nursery rhyme are set with integrity and authenticity. The song is accessible to the youngest choir and poignantly illustrates the difference between "childlike" music and "childish" music. The composer uses a variety of familiar folk rhyme melodies joined together by clever melodic interludes. The piece is composed in G major, in $\frac{4}{4}$, with a vocal range from D_4 to E_5.
Pedagogical value: The study and performance of this simple unison chorale offers young singers the opportunity to sing G major tonality, four-bar phrases, legato versus staccato articulations, and dramatic dynamic contrasts. The texts and melodies serve as comfortably familiar fare alongside new musical challenges for young voices.
Level of difficulty: Beginning; for very young choirs

Composer: Byrd, William
Title: Non Nobis Domine
Publisher: Oxford #40.023
Voicing: Three-part canon, unaccompanied
Style: Renaissance
Language: Latin
Notes: The simple melody of this piece, with a range of an octave, forms a lovely canon at the interval of a fifth. It can be pitched to accommodate the changing ranges of boys: In this edition, it is written in two keys (one for treble choirs and one for mixed choirs).
Pedagogical value: The flowing line and reverent mood of the piece can encourage controlled linear singing over a relatively wide range.
Level of difficulty: Intermediate

Composer: Carto, Thomas
Title: The Cat of Cats
Publisher: Boosey & Hawkes #6364
Voicing: Two parts, piano accompaniment
Style: Contemporary
Language: English
Notes: This charming setting of a poem about cats captures some of the mystery and reticence of the beloved beast. The accompaniment purrs gently with a haunting pattern that is based on the whole-tone scale, and a "whisper chorus" used throughout provides a pleasant contrast.
Pedagogical value: This piece is a wonderful way to introduce children to nondiatonic sonorities, as it makes use of the whole-tone scale and numerous major seconds in the piano and vocal parts. Difficult intervals are approached by step, so they are entirely accessible to young singers.
Level of difficulty: Intermediate

Composer: Carto, Thomas
Title: Muddy Puddle
Publisher: Boosey & Hawkes OC3B6363
Voicing: Three parts, unaccompanied
Style: Contemporary
Language: English
Notes: Carto has set the absurd poem by Dennis Lee in a refreshing unaccompanied style. Simple vocal ostinatos are passed between the voices to accompany the rapidly articulated text.
Pedagogical value: This piece is a delightful and musical means of improving articulation and ensemble. It ends with a challenging homophonic section and an accelerando.
Level of difficulty: Intermediate

Composer: Chass, Blanche, arr.
Title: Hanerot Halalu
Publisher: Mark Foster MF 877
Voicing: Two parts, piano accompaniment
Style: Hebrew folk
Language: Hebrew
Notes: This spirited melody, in a minor key, is accompanied by a simple vocal ostinato. Just prior to a quick-moving coda, the arrangement presents a contrasting homophonic section in which the motion slows.
Pedagogical value: The simple ostinato makes two-part singing particularly accessible. The coda offers a chance to learn about accelerando: it rushes to the end, where it culminates with a shout that the children love.
Level of difficulty: Beginning

Composer: Cockshott, Gerald, arr.
Title: Three French Carols
Publisher: Roberton Publications 312-41236
Voicing: Unison, piano or organ accompaniment
Style: French folk
Language: French/English
Notes: The first of these charming carols, "Carol of the Crib," has three verses that are sparsely accompanied by the keyboard instrument. "A Carol of Bethlehem," again with three verses, has the simplest melody of the three carols. The livelier final carol, "In Bethlehem, That Fair City," has a simple chorus of alleluias. The accompaniment supports the voice line but does not consistently double the melody.
Pedagogical value: These lovely carol melodies are pitched appropriately for light head-voice development. The repetitive texts, particularly that of the second carol, can provide children with an introduction to singing in French.
Level of difficulty: Beginning; for very young choirs

Composer: Copland, Aaron
Title: Ching-a-ring Chaw (from *Old American Songs*)
Publisher: Boosey & Hawkes 5025
Voicing: Four parts, piano accompaniment
Style: American folk
Language: English
Notes: This fast-moving setting of a minstrel song will appeal to any choir. The piece builds to a climax, then tapers off to a quiet coda where the voices pass a phrase back and forth, and ends with an unabashed shout.
Pedagogical value: Singers will learn to articulate the text deftly and to be rhythmically precise.
Level of difficulty: Advanced

Composer: Copland, Aaron; arr. Wilding-White
Title: The Little Horses (from *Old American Songs*)
Publisher: Boosey & Hawkes #5508
Voicing: Two parts, piano accompaniment
Style: American folk
Language: English
Notes: Copland's adaptation of this folk melody has been arranged for choir by Wilding-White. The accompaniment and the simple parts honor the music and text of the tender lullaby.
Pedagogical value: Learning opportunities lie in the rhythm and in the tempo and meter changes. An effective performance will require careful attention to the conductor.
Level of difficulty: Intermediate

Composer: Copland, Aaron; arr. Irving Fine
Title: Simple Gifts (from *Old American Songs*)
Publisher: Boosey & Hawkes #1903
Voicing: Two parts, piano accompaniment
Style: American folk (Shaker tune)
Language: English
Notes: Irving Fine has transcribed Copland's folk song setting and arranged it for choirs. He has preserved the harmonies Copland chose to accompany this familiar Shaker tune.
Pedagogical value: This song can provide a vehicle for learning eighth- and sixteenth-note patterns, which are typical of Shaker folk music. This is a melody worthy of children, and could be followed by listening to Copland's ballet music *Appalachian Spring*.
Level of difficulty: Beginning

Composer: Crocker, Emily, arr.
Title: Cripple Creek
Publisher: Jenson Publications, 423-03032
Voicing: Two parts (piano accompaniment optional)
Style: American folk
Language: English
Notes: This joyful setting of the familiar fiddle tune will appeal immediately to young singers. Crocker has included a short clapping interlude and numerous dynamic markings for variety and expression.
Pedagogical value: This arrangement provides easy entry for young choristers to two-part singing. In one section, the melody is passed back and forth between the two voices, and in others the second part takes on a simple accompanying line that has its own melodic character.
Level of difficulty: Beginning

Composer: Curtright, Carolee, arr.
Title: Kookaburra
Publisher: Boosey & Hawkes #6255
Voicing: Three parts, piano accompaniment
Style: American folk
Language: English
Notes: The arranger has set this familiar and well-loved round to a refreshing Mixolydian accompaniment with two vocal ostinatos. When the melody is in the lower voice, it is altered to accommodate the limited-range singer.
Pedagogical value: This piece is a great vehicle for easing children into part singing and for practicing the expressive potential of dynamics.
Level of difficulty: Beginning

Composer: Davidson, Charles
Title: Dance with Me (from *Singing of Angels*)
Publisher: MCA Music #UC38
Voicing: Three parts, piano accompaniment
Style: Contemporary
Language: English
Notes: This song begins, as the title suggests, with a dance in a quick triple meter. The compelling meter and rhythm propel the motion forward toward the dramatic coda. There, the words "remember me," rendered at a slower tempo and hushed dynamic level, remind us of the Jewish children to whom the song is dedicated and who "dance only in our memories."
Pedagogical value: With this appealing selection, the singers can develop the skill of singing parallel thirds and sixths, and a sense of the expressive elements that contribute to dramatic effects.
Level of difficulty: Intermediate

Composer: Davidson, Charles
Title: In the Valley (from *Singing of Angels*)
Publisher: MCA Music #UC40
Voicing: Three parts, piano accompaniment
Style: Contemporary
Language: English
Notes: Children adore songs with accelerandos, and after alternating sections with slower and faster tempos, this one makes a race for the double bar and a shouted "Maz'1 Tov!" (Good Luck!). The text is about a happy Jewish family who collect children and animals—complete with their sounds.
Pedagogical value: This piece is useful for developing rhythmic skills. Changes of meter from double to triple provide learning opportunities, as does learning to control the piece's accelerando.
Level of difficulty: Beginning; for very young choirs

Composer: DeCormier, Robert, arr.
Title: The Erie Canal
Publisher: Lawson-Gould #352073
Voicing: Two parts, piano and percussion accompaniment
Style: American folk
Language: English
Notes: This traditional work song has immediate appeal to young choirs in part because of the syncopation and swinging rhythms. This aspect of the melody has inspired a blues-style piano accompaniment.
Pedagogical value: This song can provide a nice lesson in style. The contrapuntal vocal parts are accessible; choirs with minimal part singing experience will succeed at this piece.
Level of difficulty: Beginning; for very young choirs

Composer: De Lassus, Rolande; arr. Doreen Rao
Title: Musica Dei donum optimi
Publisher: Boosey & Hawkes OC4B6449
Voicing: Four-part canon, unaccompanied
Style: Renaissance
Language: Latin

Notes: The expressive vocal line encompasses an octave and a fifth (A_3 to E_5). With the exception of ascending octave leaps, it moves downward by step and thirds. De Lassus achieves tension in the smooth, sustained phrases with the suspensions typical of this period.

Pedagogical value: This canon can provide an introduction to counterpoint and an accessible introduction to the word-painting techniques of the Renaissance.

Level of difficulty: Intermediate

Composer: Drynan, Margaret
Title: Songs for Judith
Publisher: Gordon V. Thompson Music
Voicing: Unison, piano accompaniment
Style: Contemporary
Language: English

Notes: These are four songs that contrast in style and form a lovely set. They range from C_4 to E_5. "Lullaby" (first two verses anonymous, third verse by the composer) is the longest. The second song, "Choosing Shoes" (poem by Frieda Wolfe), consists of through-composed, four-bar verses that tell of the excitement of buying new shoes. The piano keeps the excitement going with running eighth notes, until the last, minor verse, which describes the "wipe-them-on-the-mat shoes" (in accented notes) that they'll buy. In the very short song "Sh" (verse by S. Tippet), Mother and Father remind the child that "running in the hall is a very great bother" and that "Missus Grumpy Grundy, who lives down below, will come right up!" "Little" (verse by Dorothy Aldis) is also very short: a lilting setting of a poem in which the child sings of her baby brother, who is still too little to look when she shows her doll and her book.

Pedagogical value: These songs are excellent for the very youngest children, while still providing a challenge in singing in tune and good singing for older children. Sudden changes in dynamics, tempo, and expression are used throughout the four songs.

Level of difficulty: Beginning; for very young choirs

Composer: Dvorak, Antonin
Title: The Dove and the Maple Tree (Op. 32, No. 1)
Publisher: Walton Music WH-141
Voicing: Two parts, piano accompaniment
Style: Romantic
Language: Czech/English
Notes: This stirring music is rich with the sounds of Moravian folk music. The role of the piano is equal in importance to that of the vocal lines.
Pedagogical value: The voice parts move in parallel thirds and sixths with occasional chromatic alterations within and between the two voices. This duet will offer children a chance to hear and practice this harmonic style, which is so typical of Czech folk music.
Level of difficulty: Intermediate

Composer: Dvorak, Antonin
Title: Flow, Danube, Ebb and Flow
Publisher: Walton Music
Voicing: Two parts, piano accompaniment
Style: Romantic
Language: Czech/English
Notes: This stirring music is rich with the sounds of Moravian folk music. The role of the piano is equal in importance to that of the vocal lines.
Pedagogical value: The voice parts move in parallel thirds and sixths, with occasional chromatic alterations within and betwen the two voices. This duet will offer children a chance to hear and sing in tune these harmonies so typical of Czech folk music.
Level of difficulty: Intermediate

Composer: Elliott, David
Title: The Shenandoah Blues
Publisher: Boosey & Hawkes OC 2B6455
Voicing: Two parts, piano (optional jazz combo available)
Style: Contemporary (jazz)
Language: English
Notes: This piece was written to familiarize students with the elements of jazz style by contrasting a familiar melody with a jazz version of same. Either before or after introducing "The Shenandoah Blues," the teacher may wish to invite students to suggest ways of "jazzing up" the traditional "O Shenandoah" tune and to compare and contrast their versions with this setting.
Pedagogical value: This piece offers an excellent contrast between the folk style of the original song, "O Shenandoah," and the jazz elements of this arrangement. The edition includes a musical analysis and teaching suggestions.
Level of difficulty: Intermediate

Composer: Fallis, Lois T., and Ruth Watson Henderson
Title: Cinderella (A Musical Playlet in Two Acts) (from the collection *...and a Glass Slipper*)
Publisher: Waterloo Music Company ISBN 0-88909-047-5 (Canada)
Voicing: Unison, piano accompaniment
Style: Contemporary
Language: English
Notes: The accompaniments for this playlet were written by Ruth Watson Henderson, with the texts by Lois Fallis. The range is from C_4 to $E\flat_5$. This is a delightful, very easy collection of eleven pieces that even the very youngest children can learn quickly and that all children will love. The pieces include one piano solo ("Music at the Ball") and two choral speeches.
Pedagogical value: Though the pieces are easy, there are many musical concepts that may be taught through these pieces, such as canon (the introductory piece is a three-part canon in $\frac{5}{8}$), the minor mode, first and second endings, and dynamic contrasts. Solo opportunities for Cinderella, the two stepsisters, the fairy godmother, and the prince are short enough that they can be shared in rehearsal, with many children getting a chance to sing a solo.
Level of difficulty: Beginning; for very young choirs

Composer: Fauré, Gabriel
Title: Messe basse
Publisher: Theodore Presser
Voicing: Two parts, organ accompaniment
Style: Contemporary
Language: Latin
Notes: Fauré has set four parts of the Mass in this reverent and reflective work. Two movements feature solo voice with choral responses and accompaniment. The "Sanctus" and "Agnus Dei" are written for first and second sopranos. The "Agnus Dei" is often programmed alone.
Pedagogical value: With these intense and expressive lyrical lines, children learn to shape phrases. Handling the chromaticism that Fauré used in the development of melodic ideas facilitates sensitivity to harmonic shifts.
Level of difficulty: Intermediate

Composer: Felciano, Richard
Title: Rocking
Publisher: Marks Music #4512
Voicing: Two parts, unaccompanied
Style: Czechoslovakian folk (seasonal)
Language: English
Notes: This familiar Czech carol is set with a careful simplicity that fits the childlike text of the lullaby. In the first section, the second voice shares the text with the melody; in the second, the lower voice moves independently with the repeated phrase, "rock you."
Pedagogical value: The simple carol can encourage light, quiet singing. In learning the ending, the children experience a "molto rallentando." Felciano has written a number of fine works for children's choirs; additional titles by this composer should be considered.
Level of difficulty: Beginning; for very young choirs

Composer: Finzi, Gerald
Title: Dead in the Cold (No. 5 from *Ten Children's Songs,* Op. 1)
Publisher: Boosey & Hawkes #6149
Voicing: Two parts, piano accompaniment
Style: Contemporary
Language: English
Notes: The title of this piece might scare directors off, but a close look reveals a beautiful musical moment. The Christina Rossetti text is about a bird found in the snow. Like other music by this composer, the lyrical quality of this choral draws children and audiences alike to its beauty.
Pedagogical value: The carefully hewn phrases and the imitative counterpoint contribute to the piece's poignant expression—expression that is entirely appropriate for children and appealing to them.
Level of difficulty: Intermediate

Composer: Finzi, Gerald
Title: Lullaby, O Lullaby (No. 3 from *Ten Children's Songs,* Op. 1)
Publisher: Boosey & Hawkes #6147
Voicing: Unison, piano accompaniment
Style: Contemporary
Language: English
Notes: This tender, simple lullaby is ideal for beginning choirs. New text and melodies alternate with the phrase, "Lullaby, O Lullaby." The composer suggests having individuals sing the alternate phrases for contrast.
Pedagogical value: The repetition of the title phrase throughout provides a chance to focus on accurate singing of the repeated pitch pattern, a limited number of vowel sounds, and artistic phrasing.
Level of difficulty: Beginning; for very young choirs

Composer: Finzi, Gerald
Title: Margaret Has a Milking Pail (No. 6 from *Ten Children's Songs*, Op. 1)
Publisher: Boosey & Hawkes #6150
Voicing: Two parts, piano accompaniment
Style: Contemporary
Language: English
Notes: This little piece is over before you know it. It moves at a fast clip, requiring quick articulation of text. The poem talks of life at another time (using words like "threshing flail" and "betimes"), and the music captures this spirit as well.
Pedagogical value: The two voices, which zip along in imitation, require clean and facile diction.
Level of difficulty: Beginning

Composer: Fitzgerald, Ella, and Al Feldman; arr. David Elliott
Title: A-Tisket, A-Tasket
Publisher: Boosey & Hawkes OC3B6456
Voicing: Three parts, piano (optional jazz combo available)
Style: Contemporary
Language: English
Notes: This arrangement was written for the twentieth anniversary season of the Glen Ellyn Children's Chorus. A jazz rhythm section accompaniment is available from the publisher; the piano/vocal version is suitable for both rehearsal and performance when bass and drums are not available. The "walking" style for the left hand in the piano part serves to anchor the rhythm of the entire piece.
Pedagogical value: Rehearsing and performing this piece allows young choristers to experience authentic jazz style, an important part of their American music heritage. Students should be made aware of the "time," swing "feel," and the accents that are characteristics of this style. This arrangement offers students the opportunity to learn scat singing in the style of American vocal artist Ella Fitzgerald.
Level of difficulty: Intermediate

Composer: Floyd, Carlisle
Title: Long Long Ago
Publisher: Boosey & Hawkes #5648
Voicing: Two parts, piano accompaniment
Style: Contemporary
Language: English
Notes: Floyd has composed a very simple melodic motive and developed it into a beautiful, singable melody. The music lies perfectly for children's voices.
Pedagogical value: The clear ABA' form, the changing meter, the slightly complex and dissonant sound, and the imitative texture provide many opportunities for developing vocal skill and musical understanding.
Level of difficulty: Intermediate

Composer: Floyd, Carlisle
Title: Two Stephenson Songs
Publisher: Boosey & Hawkes #5627
Voicing: Unison, piano accompaniment
Style: Contemporary
Language: English
Notes: These two short pieces center around a short, repeated melodic motive. In the first, "Rain," raindrops are portrayed in the staccato treatment of the text and in the accompaniment. The second, "Where Go the Boats?" is legato, with a wavelike pattern in the piano.
Pedagogical value: Both of these songs have changes of meter. The principle of meter signatures can be illustrated in the second song, which alternates between $\frac{6}{4}$ and $\frac{8}{4}$ and ends with a measure of $\frac{10}{4}$.
Level of difficulty: Beginning; for very young choirs

Composer: Forsyth, Malcolm
Title: Three Zulu Songs
Publisher: Gordon V. Thompson Music G-333
Voicing: Three parts, flute, oboe, and drums
Style: Contemporary
Language: Zulu
Notes: This is a three-movement work written on poems by the famous Zulu poet, Benedict W. Vilakazi. The vocal material of this work is made up of imitative and repeated traditional melodies rhythmically derived from African models and cleverly composed in a tasteful contemporary manner. The authentic Zulu language is preserved: the edition offers special remarks on Zulu pronunciation, and there is also a guide to the many "clicking" sounds of the Zulu language. The music includes very singable melodies, clapping, and unusual contrasts between the flute and oboe material.
Pedagogical value: It is important for young singers to have the opportunity to study and perform music characteristic of many peoples in many lands. Singing in the Zulu language and in a contemporary setting of traditional Zulu songs, young choirs learn the sounds of a new language, plus the rhythmic and melodic qualities characteristic of Zulu culture.
Level of difficulty: Advanced

Composer: Foster, Anthony, arr.
Title: Two Tongue-Twisters
Publisher: Oxford University Press #81-046
Voicing: Unison, piano accompaniment
Style: Contemporary
Language: English
Notes: These two tongue twisters will fill the bill of novelty pieces. The first, "Betty Botter's Butter," is the more difficult of the two, with its unexpected turns and leaps. The inane and delightful "Moses' Toeses" is simpler.
Pedagogical value: Both of these are excellent selections for improving diction; the careful articulation of the b's and t's in the first song and the sibilants in the second will have long-lasting effects. For developing concept and reading skills, "Betty Botter's Butter" offers an ascending melodic sequence that repeats a third higher. In "Moses," the triple-meter melody ends with a dramatic crescendo and a fermata.
Level of difficulty: Beginning; for very young choirs

Composer: Franck, Melchior; arr. Mary Goetze
Title: Da pacem Domine
Publisher: Boosey & Hawkes #6187
Voicing: Four parts, unaccompanied
Style: Renaissance
Language: Latin
Notes: The Franck "Da pacem Domine" is a simple canon at the fourth, which can be sung in two or four parts. This arrangement grows from the unison statement of the melody to a two- and then four-voice canon then four-voice canon.
Pedagogical value: The melody encompasses a range of a fifth and progresses by small intervals, thus providing easy entry into a contrapuntal texture that sounds more complex than it is.
Level of difficulty: Beginning; for very young choirs

Composer: Gabrieli, Andrea
Title: Ave Maria
Publisher: Alexander Broude AB999
Voicing: Three parts, unaccompanied
Style: Renaissance
Language: Latin
Notes: This setting reflects the crossover in style from the late Renaissance to the early Baroque. Part of the composition is polyphonic and part homophonic; the setting would be effective with string or recorder accompaniment.
Pedagogical value: This piece demands vocal independence on the part of the singers. The Latin text provides extended opportunities to gain pure and uniform vowel production. The work demands equal balancing of the parts. There is a wide range between the soprano and the lower voices that poses a challenge to advanced choirs.
Level of difficulty: Intermediate

Composer: Gershwin, George, and Ira Gershwin; arr. Kirby Shaw
Title: Strike Up the Band (from *My One and Only*)
Publisher: Warner Brothers #441-19192
Voicing: Two parts, piano accompaniment
Style: Contemporary
Language: English
Notes: Shaw's arrangement of Gershwin's familiar tune stays very close to the original song. The piano accompaniment imitates a snare drum (referred to in the text). The form is A-B-C-coda: The A section begins in unison, goes to a call and response, and ends in two equal parts. Singers scat-sing in section B, and in section C the soprano and alto lines share the melody.
Pedagogical value: This tune provides students with an opportunity to sing in the theater/Broadway style—simple choreography would be appropriate. The B section offers an excellent opportunity for the children to experience scat singing.
Level of difficulty: Intermediate

Composer: Gevaert, François; arr. Walter Ehret
Title: The Sleep of the Child Jesus
Publisher: Spratt Music Publishers #CCS633
Voicing: Three parts, piano accompaniment
Style: French folk (seasonal)
Language: English
Notes: This work has a wonderful quality of the French Noël. The three verses are written in a straightforward manner with the upper voices acting as a vocal obbligato in the second verse. The soprano and alto parts are essentially the same in the first and third verses. The quality of the lullaby is especially lovely, as it is set in the key of F minor with a final cadence in F major.
Pedagogical value: The peaceful quality of this lullaby requires pianissimo singing from the young singers. The second verse provides opportunities for the second sopranos and the altos to share the melody line.
Level of difficulty: Intermediate

Composer: Goetze, Mary, arr.

Title: Ca' the Yowes

Publisher: Boosey & Hawkes #6258

Voicing: Two parts, piano and recorder accompaniment

Style: Scottish folk

Language: English

Notes: This Scottish folk song is accompanied by a simple countermelody, which is both sung and played on the recorder. The arrangement's opening motive becomes the theme for a bird song played on recorder during the second verse. A helpful pronunciation and translation guide is provided.

Pedagogical value: This arrangement gives singers an introduction to the charm and lyrical character of Scottish melody. It provides an opportunity for young singers to develop a sense of phrasing, to develop vocal control over leaps, and to experience two-part singing in a contrapuntal texture.

Level of difficulty: Beginning

Composer: Goetze, Mary, arr.

Title: Crawdad Hole

Publisher: Boosey & Hawkes #6184

Voicing: Three parts, unaccompanied

Style: American folk

Language: English

Notes: Goetze's arrangement provides young singers an opportunity to sing parts that are easily accessible and interesting to learn. This energetic and humorous folk song is sung by the middle voice, accompanied by two repetitive countermelodies. The opening is stated in a quasi-recitative style.

Pedagogical value: This appealing folk song is a novelty piece that will delight singers and audiences alike. The part writing gives young singers an opportunity to develop skills for singing inner voice parts.

Level of difficulty: Intermediate

Composer: Goetze, Mary, arr.

Title: Dormi, Dormi (Sweetly Slumber)

Publisher: Boosey & Hawkes OCUB6128

Voicing: Unison, piano or harp accompaniment

Style: Italian folk (seasonal)

Language: Italian/English

Notes: This Italian/English carol is in F major, with a range from E_4 to C_5. There are two verses, both in $\frac{2}{4}$; the choruses are sung in a lilting $\frac{6}{8}$ (the eighth note remains constant). The piano accompaniment is marked "quietly, flowing," in the verses, flowing easily with eighth-note melodic open fifths in ascending octaves. The voice sustains a lovely legato melody in easy quarter-note rhythms. The "fa-la-la" sequences are doubled by the piano accompaniment. Dotted quarter-note patterns in the bass serve to keep the line sustained.

Pedagogical value: This is a beautiful carol that works well for young voices and lends itself to an expressive, legato performance. The melody may take some time for the youngest children to learn, and all children will need to work on good intonation. Contrasts between simple and compound meter might be discussed. The Italian text is easy to sing.

Level of difficulty: Beginning; for very young choirs

Composer: Goetze, Mary, arr.

Title: The Little Birch Tree

Publisher: Boosey & Hawkes #6130

Voicing: Unison, piano accompaniment (optional flute or recorder)

Style: Russian folk

Language: English

Notes: This piece is in E minor, in $\frac{2}{4}$ time, with a range from E_4 to D_5. It is strophic, in four verses, with a through-composed piano accompaniment and short interludes between the verses. The piano uses octave tremolos in the third verse to imitate a *balalaika*.

Pedagogical value: This is a very simple, flowing melody in a beautiful setting. The melodic line is very limited in range, staying mainly within the lower fifth of the minor scale. Discussion might include the instruments in the song (flute and *balalaika*), how the piano imitates them, and how the voice and piano imitate the sound of the wind, and folk songs in general.

Level of difficulty: Beginning; for very young choirs

Composer: Goetze, Mary, arr.
Title: The Old Carrion Crow
Publisher: Boosey & Hawkes #OC2B365
Voicing: Two parts, piano accompaniment
Style: Canadian folk
Language: English
Notes: Set in the Dorian mode, this Nova Scotian folk song tells an amusing story, which is interspersed with appealing responses and a chorus of nonsense syllables. Dissonance is created by an interesting and active piano accompaniment that departs from the scale of the melody.
Pedagogical value: Young singers will concentrate on diction, particularly the consonants used in the section of nonsense syllables. The intervals found in this piece offer an opportunity to focus on intonation skills.
Level of difficulty: Beginning

Composer: Goetze, Mary, arr.
Title: Old Joe Clark
Publisher: Boosey & Hawkes #6125
Voicing: Three parts, unaccompanied
Style: American folk
Language: English
Notes: This familiar American fiddle tune is arranged in a playful setting that captures the flavor of the jocular text. This lively Mixolydian folk song is accessible: the first soprano, second soprano, and alto lines all have interesting and singable parts. Scat singing (pling pling-a-pling) adds to the rhythmic interest, helping to make this tune exciting for the singer and audience alike.
Pedagogical value: Goetze's arrangement is accessible and interesting to children because of the uniqueness of each individual part. By singing this tune, each child acquires the ability to sing independently and with good intonation and gains a better understanding of our American culture.
Level of difficulty: Intermediate

Composer: Goetze, Mary, arr.
Title: The Piglets' Christmas
Publisher: Boosey & Hawkes #OCUB6402
Voicing: Unison, piano accompaniment
Style: American folk (seasonal)
Language: English
Notes: This charming, simple Appalachian folk song about a warm-hearted farmer has been freely adapted to become a secular Christmas song. The Mixolydian accompaniment ventures beyond diatonicism to accompany the stepwise melody. Embedded in the piano part are quotations of a familiar carol that has been altered in mode and in meter.
Pedagogical value: The stepwise rise and fall of the lovely melody line require good intonation skills. The repeated "tra la la" section of the folk song provides the student with opportunities to concentrate on the production of the open "ah" vowel sound. This tune would be an excellent vehicle for building sight-reading for the young choir.
Level of difficulty: Beginning; for very young choirs

Composer: Grandi, Alesandro
Title: Hodie, nobis de caelo
Publisher: Mark Foster #803
Voicing: Two parts, piano accompaniment
Style: Baroque
Language: Latin
Notes: An excellent example of early Italian Baroque music, this edition offers a realization of the continuo that supports the very elaborate vocal line.
Pedagogical value: Singers are introduced to Latin text. Also, students will experience the feel of triple versus duple meter.
Level of difficulty: Intermediate

Composer: Grieg, Edvard
Title: Three Songs
Publisher: Hinshaw Music HMC–401
Voicing: Two parts, piano accompaniment
Style: Romantic
Language: English
Notes: In these songs, Grieg captures an essential element in Romantic thought: the glorification of nature. In folk-song fashion, these pieces portray the spirit of man dealing with his surroundings. "The Hunter" uses the open fifth to depict the hunting horn; "The Boatman" uses a running sixteenth-note pattern to illustrate running water and "The Woodsman" captures the rollicking motion of the hunter.
Pedagogical value: These melodies expose the young singer to vocal imagery. Diction can be emphasized while students experience these lovely pieces.
Level of difficulty: Intermediate

Composer: Grundman, Clare, arr.
Title: Pat-A-Pan
Publisher: Boosey & Hawkes #6040
Voicing: Two parts, piano, flute, drum
Style: French folk (seasonal)
Language: English
Notes: This Burgundian folk song is adapted by the well-known band arranger, Clare Grundman. Grundman writes a very lively piano accompaniment using verse and refrain with flute obbligato and snare drum accompaniment.
Pedagogical value: Diction should be stressed in this piece, especially explosive consonants. Accuracy of rhythm should also be emphasized.
Level of difficulty: Beginning; for very young choirs

Composer: Grundman, Clare
Title: Zoo Illogical
Publisher: Boosey & Hawkes #5855
Voicing: Unison, piano accompaniment
Style: Contemporary
Language: English
Notes: These five character pieces are beautifully crafted by the well-known American composer Clare Grundman. Grundman has succeeded in setting an imaginative musical description of animals: the mongoose, the anteater, the llama, the giraffe, and the hippo. The pieces are energetic, humorous, and appealing to elementary-aged children. The combined short movements create a mini-extended work.

Pedagogical value: These "animal" pieces can serve as an educational companion to Saint-Saëns' *Carnival of the Animals*. Learning diction skills is made fun with the use of tongue-twisting lines and humorous texts, and the use of changing meter provides an additional challenge. This is an ideal addition to any concert.

Level of difficulty: Beginning; for very young choirs

Composer: Hall, William D., arr.
Title: I Know Where I'm Goin'
Publisher: National Music Publishers WHC Series No. 1
Voicing: Two parts, piano (optional flute, oboe, or melodica)
Style: American folk
Language: English
Notes: The first two verses of this setting are through-composed, in the key of G major; the coda shifts to B major and changes meter from $\frac{4}{4}$ to $\frac{3}{2}$. The coda climaxes with a short trio between two voices and the flute.

Pedagogical value: With the lovely "strumming accompaniment," the singers can experience cantabile singing by making use of sustained breath control. Independence of the two parts, the various meter changes, and a beautiful unaccompanied section make this an especially valued teaching piece.

Level of difficulty: Beginning; for very young choirs

Composer: Handel, George Frideric
Title: The Lord Is My Strength
Publisher: National Music #WHC-147
Voicing: Two parts, piano accompaniment
Style: Baroque
Language: English
Notes: This challenging work reflects Handel's mature vocal style in a very ornate, melismatic setting of the words. It is a lovely duet that one might find, typically, in Handel's secular cantatas.
Pedagogical value: Students experience the minor tonality in singing this work—providing a challenge to their intonation skills. The work introduces triplet and thirty-second note patterns, requiring vocal flexibility and careful rhythmic ensemble.
Level of difficulty: Intermediate

Composer: Handel, George Frideric
Title: O Let the Merry Bells Ring
Publisher: Boosey & Hawkes OCUB6509
Voicing: Unison, piano accompaniment
Style: Baroque
Language: English
Notes: This well-known Handel aria is easily sung by unison children's choir. The descending D major scale pattern establishes the bell-ringing motive that is developed and embellished throughout the song. The imitative piano accompaniment and the triple dance rhythms make this song an interesting lesson in Baroque word painting.
Pedagogical value: The dancelike melody, rhythmic piano accompaniment and simple harmonic structure provide many learning opportunities for young choirs. The study and performance of Handel melodies teaches choristers to sustain pitch, articulate rhythms, and understand simple song forms. This unison song may be performed by large ensemble, small ensemble, unison, or solo voice.
Level of difficulty: Intermediate

Composer: Handel, George Frideric
Title: O Lovely Peace, with Plenty Crown'd (from *Judas Maccabaeus*)
Publisher: E. C. Schirmer #1039
Voicing: Two parts, piano accompaniment
Style: Baroque
Language: English
Notes: This pastorale is an example of the composer's characteristic use of word painting. It is typical of the love duets found in the secular Italian cantatas. The soprano and alto lines move independently as well as homophonically.
Pedagogical value: Handel gives us a beautiful lyrical line, which is a good introduction to imitative counterpoint. The neumatic text setting is wonderful for highlighting vocal flexibility.
Level of difficulty: Intermediate

Composer: Handel, George Frideric
Title: Thanks Be to Thee
Publisher: Plymouth Music
Voicing: Two parts, piano accompaniment
Style: Baroque
Language: English
Notes: This thanksgiving ode begins in unison. The unison statement is followed by a two-part section in which the second voice is simply a lower obbligato accompanying the melody.
Pedagogical value: This is an excellent piece for teaching the breath control needed for sustaining long musical lines. This piece also aids students in the study of English diction skills.
Level of difficulty: Beginning

Composer: Handel, George Frideric
Title: Where'er You Walk
Publisher: Boosey & Hawkes OCUB6510
Voicing: Unison, piano accompaniment
Style: Baroque
Language: English
Notes: This well-known Handel aria is easily sung by unison children's choir. The smooth melodic line, sung over the walking bass figure in the piano accompaniment, serves as an interesting lesson in Baroque word painting. This edition is set in the same key as the original and requires supported head-voice singing.
Pedagogical value: The singable melody, walking rhythm patterns, and simple harmonic structure provide many learning opportunities for young choirs. Its study and performance teaches choristers to sustain pitch, articulate rhythms, and understand simple song forms. This unison song may be performed by large ensemble, small ensemble, unison, or solo voice.
Level of difficulty: Intermediate

Composer: Hardwicke, Arthur, arr.
Title: Old Man Noah
Publisher: Pro Art Belwin Mills Pro Ch. 2934
Voicing: Two parts, piano accompaniment
Style: American folk
Language: English
Notes: This humorous and lively sea chantey is great fun. The two verses are written in a simple echo style, and the refrain is voiced in two parts, accessible to the beginning singer.
Pedagogical value: "Old Man Noah" would be an excellent selection for developing crisp diction and the interpretation of dynamic contrasts. It is a fun, humorous tune that the younger choir will enjoy.
Level of difficulty: Intermediate

Composer: Hawkins, Walter; arr. Martin Sirvatka
Title: I'm Goin' Up a Yonder
Publisher: Boosey & Hawkes OC4B6451
Voicing: Four parts, piano accompaniment
Style: Contemporary (gospel)
Language: English
Notes: This popular gospel tune starts with a solo voice and continues to build in texture and dynamic, climaxing with the addition of a soaring descant. The call-and-response form builds an ever-increasing sense of expectation. The repetition of the text, "I'm goin' up a yonder," helps to amplify the longing to go "home."
Pedagogical value: The simple harmonic progression provides singers with early success in part singing. This piece provides students with the opportunity to develop an understanding of gospel-style singing, including the use of blues notes, free-time relationships, and call-and-response. The edition includes editorial notes with teaching suggestions.
Level of difficulty: Intermediate

Composer: Henderson, Ruth Watson
Title: A la ferme (from *Through the Eyes of Children*)
Publisher: Gordon V. Thompson Music #G-178
Voicing: Unison, piano accompaniment
Style: Contemporary
Language: French
Notes: This is a wonderful, folklike tune that is an excellent example of strophic treatment of text. The lively accompaniment adds texture and charm to the beauty of the line.
Pedagogical value: This lovely chorale introduces children to the principles of French diction as well as changing meter.
Level of difficulty: Beginning

Composer: Henderson, Ruth Watson
Title: Four Little Foxes (from *Musical Animal Tales, Set V*)
Publisher: Gordon V. Thompson Music G-321
Voicing: Three parts, piano accompaniment
Style: Contemporary
Language: English
Notes: Based on a text by Lew Sarett, this sensitive three-part composition explores four verses of dynamic poetry in polyphonic, imitative style. The story of newborn foxes who lost their mother in the hunter's trap poignantly weaves an exquisite literary-musical web around the moral issues of the environment today.
Pedagogical value: There is educational value in simple exposure to this music, in which words and music are married in a highly artistic manner. The inherent drama, felt by the conductor and choristers alike, motivates the study and performance of this work. The music is rhythmically and harmonically challenging: the $\frac{7}{8}$ measure should be conducted in a three-beat pattern (3+2+2). The use of movement, chanting, and conducting assists children in mastering the rhythmic challenges inherent in this contemporary Canadian choral work.
Level of difficulty: Advanced

Composer: Henderson, Ruth Watson
Title: Tree Toad (from *Musical Animal Tales, Set I*)
Publisher: Gordon V. Thompson Music G-166
Voicing: Unison (optional alto, piano accompaniment)
Style: Contemporary
Language: English
Notes: This is an imaginative rhythmic composition set in narrative style. The text is a humorous tongue-twister that appeals to children. Henderson composed five sets of *Musical Animal Tales* ranging from unison with piano to three-part, unaccompanied.
Pedagogical value: This piece gives young singers an excellent opportunity to demonstrate crisp diction and rhythmic contrast. This tune appeals to choristers and audience alike.
Level of difficulty: Intermediate

Composer: Henderson, Ruth Watson
Title: You'll Never Guess What I Saw (from *Through the Eyes of Children*)
Publisher: Gordon V. Thompson Music G-177
Voicing: Unison (optional second part, piano accompaniment)
Style: Contemporary
Language: English
Notes: At the beginning of this humorous piece, Henderson employs a recitation style, which is then followed by a fast, lively narrative section with an up-tempo, swing beat.
Pedagogical value: This piece can introduce the child to the experience of telling stories through choral singing. The piece uses blue notes and presents an ideal opportunity to introduce children to jazz harmonies. Crisp diction is necessary, because the center selection is written in a fast tempo.
Level of difficulty: Beginning

Composer: Holst, Gustav von
Title: The Corn Song
Publisher: E. C. Schirmer #1898
Voicing: Unison (optional second part, piano accompaniment)
Style: Contemporary
Language: English
Notes: This is an excellent example of a folk-song melody set in a modal style. It is an extremely lyrical piece on a text by John Greenleaf Whittier. The melody in the B section is accompanied by a simple and singable descant. The one-octave range is appropriate for children.
Pedagogical value: Study of the musical line in this selection results in a more lyrical approach to singing. Students must practice correct breath management. The legato melody is also an excellent opportunity to demonstrate uniformity in forming vowels.
Level of difficulty: Intermediate

Composer: Hopson, Hal, arr.
Title: Prayer for the Earth
Publisher: Augsburg Publishing 11-1745
Voicing: Two parts, handbells
Style: Russian folk
Language: English
Notes: This Russian folk tune is arranged in three verses and a coda. The anthem is written so that the unison choir and handbells or another choir (treble or adult) can perform the work antiphonally. A simple descant (Jubilate!) is optional on verse three.
Pedagogical value: A young choir can find much success with this simple folk tune. The "Jubilate" descant and coda will give young singers an opportunity to experience uniform vowel production and easy part singing. The text of "Prayer for the Earth" has a wonderful message for children and would be an effective selection on a spring concert.
Level of difficulty: Beginning; for very young choirs

Composer: Hopson, Hal
Title: Prayer of the Christmas Animals
Publisher: Shawnee Press E-5151
Voicing: Unison, piano or organ accompaniment (optional finger cymbals)
Style: Contemporary (seasonal)
Language: English
Notes: Hopson has written a charming Christmas work that is especially suitable for very young choirs. The form is ABA; a piano/organ and optional finger cymbal accompaniment supports the unison voices. The arrangement also provides opportunities for solo or small-group singing.
Pedagogical value: There is much repetition in this bright carol which would help children learn the music quickly. The ending could be sung in two parts, providing an opportunity for singing in harmony.
Level of difficulty: Beginning; for very young choirs

Composer: Hopson, Hal, arr.
Title: Twelve Gates into the City
Publisher: Mark Foster #812
Voicing: Unison (optional vocal obbligato, piano accompaniment)
Style: American folk (spiritual)
Language: English
Notes: This well-known spiritual is arranged in three verses with two refrains. A descant/obbligato may be sung with the third verse. The melody is accompanied by simple but interesting material. This carol is very accessible for young choirs.
Pedagogical value: Children respond to the melody line of this carol, and concentrating on the expressive melodic line is a natural approach to teaching this music. Shaping of the dynamics of this piece, coupled with expressing the text, make for an effective study and performance opportunity for children.
Level of difficulty: Beginning; for very young choirs

Composer: Howell, John Raymond
Title: The Angel Gabriel
Publisher: Boosey and Hawkes #6256
Voicing: Unison (optional second part, piano accompaniment)
Style: French carol
Language: English
Notes: The Basque carol has a repeated verse structure and is suitable for a relatively inexperienced treble unison choir. The optional second part at the coda may be omitted without lessening the effectiveness of the arrangement, or may be sung by just a few of the more experienced singers. Solo voices may be used for portions of verses two, three, or four. The accompaniment, including the beginning trumpet calls, is smooth and throws this simple melody into relief.
Pedagogical value: A choir can learn much from the mixed meter and lovely melodic line of this piece. There are several opportunities for singers to perform solos during the many verses of the tune, a practice that contributes to vocal independence. The simple harmony provides easy part-singing experience.
Level of difficulty: Beginning; for very young choirs

Composer: Hughes, Penelope
Title: Christmas Time
Publisher: Oxford University Press U159
Voicing: Unison, flute, glockenspiel, and percussion
Style: Contemporary (seasonal)
Language: English
Notes: This is a simple tune set in four verses and an alleluia. The flute, glockenspiel, and percussion accompaniment is simple enough for students to play.
Pedagogical value: For younger choirs, the intervals in this carol provide a challenge to sing in tune. The tempos require crisp consonants in the verses and excellent vowel alignment in the alleluia section.
Level of difficulty: Beginning

Composer: Humperdinck, Engelbert
Title: The Sandman's Song and The Children's Prayer (from *Hansel and Gretel*)
Publisher: E. C. Schirmer #1833
Voicing: Two parts, piano accompaniment
Style: Romantic
Language: English
Notes: There are numerous editions of this popular song. In the opera *Hansel and Gretel*, the prayer duet is sung by two lost and frightened children unable to find their way home in the dark. They sing in prayerful hope of being protected from the lurking dangers of the forest. The two-part vocal texture begins in homophonic style sung in thirds, then develops polyphonically in imitative style. The simplicity and innocence of this text and melody ensure that "The Children's Prayer" will remain standard repertoire for future generations.
Pedagogical value: The dramatic text and the rich harmonic colors of this duet require skilled singing in the head-voice mechanism. Vowels should be carefully vocalized, and students should understand the need for dynamic contour. The qualities of color, harmony, and dynamics found in this duet are characteristic of Romantic style—a concept that should be explored in rehearsal.
Level of difficulty: Intermediate

Composer: Ives, Charles
Title: A Christmas Carol
Publisher: Theodore Presser #342-40116
Voicing: Unison, piano accompaniment
Style: Contemporary (seasonal)
Language: English/Latin
Notes: Charles Ives wrote this lovely Christmas carol in the lilting "Sicilian" quality often found in Baroque masters such as Handel. The pastoral melody is set in unison with a coda in Latin.
Pedagogical value: The young singer will respond to the construction of this work: a legato line with a rhythmic underpinning. The carol is marked larghetto and is rhythmically challenging.
Level of difficulty: Intermediate

Composer: Jacob, Gordon
Title: Brother James' Air
Publisher: Oxford University Press #44
Voicing: Three parts, piano accompaniment
Style: English folk
Language: English
Notes: In this arrangement, verse one is sung in unison, verse two is in three parts, and verse three has a vocal obbligato. The fourth verse is arranged with the melody in the second soprano line and moving harmony lines in the outside parts. This melodic folk tune begins softly and builds throughout the piece to reach a fortissimo dynamic in the fourth verse.
Pedagogical value: This is an excellent piece for choirs to be introduced to the concept of theme and variations. Independence of parts can be emphasized throughout the three variations.
Level of difficulty: Intermediate

Composer: James, Will
Title: Alleluia
Publisher: H. T. FitzSimons #3083
Voicing: Three parts, unaccompanied
Style: Contemporary
Language: Latin
Notes: This piece of vocal chamber music develops polyphonically. The alleluia refrain could be used effectively at the end of a sacred text that cadences in G major, as an opening for a holiday program, or as an encore.
Pedagogical value: The dynamic contrast, the rhythmic interest, and the key changes of this piece make it an excellent choice for teaching young choirs. The students must be able to sing each line independently and in tune.
Level of difficulty: Intermediate

Composer: Jenkyns, Peter
Title: Bessie, The Black Cat
Publisher: Elkin & Co. 16 0110 05 (Canada)
Voicing: Unison, piano accompaniment
Style: Contemporary
Language: English
Notes: The text for this song was written by the composer. The piece is in E♭ major, in $\frac{4}{4}$; it is strophic, in four verses, with piano interludes.
Pedagogical value: This song is a little easier than "Snakes" and "The Crocodile" (also by Jenkyns), as the verses are shorter and the words a little easier to learn. The last verse begins in E♭ minor and ends in E♭ major, with melodic variations in the minor section. The dotted-eighth-note and sixteenth-note rhythms used throughout the piece are a challenge to legato singing and intonation (in the case of some of the melody's sixteenth notes).
Level of difficulty: Beginning; for very young choirs

Composer: Jenkyns, Peter
Title: The Crocodile
Publisher: Novello 19091 Cat. No. 16 0070 02
Voicing: Unison, piano accompaniment
Style: Contemporary
Language: English
Notes: The text of this piece was written by the composer. It is in G minor, in $\frac{6}{8}$, with a range from D_4 to D_5. It is strophic, in four verses. The accompaniment is through-composed, with short interludes between the verses.
Pedagogical value: The words of this piece appeal to children. An added novelty is the use of the minor mode to add to the "dread" of the subject. The incorporation of chromatic motion in the third phrase and slight rhythmic differences between the verses make this piece fairly challenging for young children.
Level of difficulty: Beginning; for very young choirs

Composer: Jenkyns, Peter
Title: Snakes
Publisher: Elkins & Co. E O 2769 (Canada)
Voicing: Unison, piano accompaniment
Style: Contemporary
Language: English
Notes: The text for this song was written by the composer. It is in E♭ major, in $\frac{12}{8}$ time, with a range from E♭$_4$ to D_5. The song is strophic, in four verses, using a through-composed accompaniment with short interludes between the verses. Many harmonic sixths and sevenths add to the overall jazzy effect.
Pedagogical value: The discussion of different types of snakes and their dangers has great appeal for young children and will carry them through learning four verses of text. This song offers a good opportunity to work on articulation and expressiveness while asking that the children maintain a proper singing tone.
Level of difficulty: Beginning; for very young choirs

Composer: Jennings, Carolyn
Title: Carol of the Cuckoo
Publisher: Choristers Guild #A-228
Voicing: Unison (optional second part, flute, and piano accompaniment)
Style: Contemporary
Language: English
Notes: This sweet Christmas song about a bird's visit to the manger is perfect for beginning singers. Although the melody repeats throughout, the composer has skillfully employed numerous means to achieve contrast: variation of the pitches, rhythm, and tempo; and the addition of instruments and a second vocal line.
Pedagogical value: For singers just learning to form a beautiful "oo" vowel, the repetitious "cuckoo" motive provides a musical means to practice it. In the middle section, the melody is sung in augmentation, followed by an accelerando and gradual return to the first tempo.
Level of difficulty: Beginning; for very young choirs

Composer: Jennings, Carolyn
Title: Cat and Mouse
Publisher: G. Schirmer #48277c
Voicing: Two and three parts, piano accompaniment
Style: Contemporary
Language: English
Notes: Jennings has set four of John Ciardi's poems about cats that children are bound to enjoy. The text is set carefully, and the character of each is reflected in the melody and accompaniment. For instance, the melody for "My Cat, Mrs. Lick-a-chin" flows above smooth arpeggios, while a more disjunct "Chang McTang McQuarter Cat" is set against a crisp staccato eight note pattern. The four make a charming set, or any one can be performed alone.
Pedagogical value: Teaching opportunities abound in these pieces. In "I Wouldn't," a waltz that offers no chances to breathe, children will learn about phrase lengths and how to stagger their breathing. In the second piece, the syllabic first section can be contrasted with the slurs in the second section. Changes in tempo and expressive ritard appear throughout.
Level of difficulty: Beginning; for very young choirs

Composer: Jordanoff, Christine, arr.
Title: Appalachian Suite I & II
Publisher: Boosey & Hawkes OCTB6522; OCTB6523
Voicing: Three parts, piano accompaniment
Style: American folk
Language: English
Notes: The simplicity and spontaneity of the American play-party game have inspired this medley of songs common to the Appalachian Mountains and many southern states. The independent melodies and simple part singing make this choral very appealing and appropriate for young choirs.
Pedagogical value: In each suite there is a variety of well-known songs that lend themselves to choreography, staging, and costuming. The folk material invites the study of its origins and its cultural context. Because of the nature of the song/games, this work can be satisfying for young treble choirs.
Level of difficulty: Intermediate

Composer: Jothen, Michael
Title: God Made Me
Publisher: Bechenhorst Press BP1016
Voicing: Unison, piano accompaniment
Style: Contemporary
Language: English
Notes: This bright anthem is written in ABA form with a simple coda. The A section has syncopated rhythms in a quick tempo; the B section is legato and is set at a slightly slower tempo. The piano accompaniment adds interest and vitality to the easily singable tune.
Pedagogical value: A young choir will enjoy this energetic tune. The diction must be crisp and clear, and the singers will learn dynamic contrast and experience ABA form. The work is written in F major, beginning on C_4, so young students can practice singing lower pitches in head voice or upper register.
Level of difficulty: Beginning

Composer: Kabalevsky, Dmitri; arr. Doreen Rao
Title: Good Night
Publisher: Boosey & Hawkes #OCUB6441
Voicing: Two parts, piano accompaniment (optional Orff instruments)
Style: Contemporary
Language: English
Notes: During the ISME World Conference in 1966, Dmitri Kabelevsky taught this song to Doreen Rao, who dedicated the arrangement to the late composer for his lifelong commitment to the music education of children around the world. The piece was first performed at the American Orff-Schulwerk National Conference in Chicago on November 13, 1987. The minor modal quality, simple English text and two-part imitative divisi make this piece an accessible and enjoyable choral experience.
Pedagogical value: The study and performance of this simple and folklike Russian song offers young singers the opportunity to experience an unusually expressive D minor melody, which is organized in two-bar phrases and varied by the octave. The piano accompaniment is written for student pianists. Solo instruments including flute, recorder, or oboe can be added to the countermelody found in the piano part.
Level of difficulty: Beginning; for very young choirs

Composer: Kennedy, John Brodbin
Title: Little Lamb, Who Made Thee?
Publisher: Boosey and Hawkes #5653
Voicing: Two parts, piano accompaniment
Style: Contemporary
Language: English
Notes: This piece has a simple and flowing melodic line and lovely piano accompaniment. The soprano and alto parts remain the same throughout the four verses of the composition. Kennedy modulates in the third and fourth verses to add interest. The fourth verse begins on a "hum," but ends with the text.
Pedagogical value: This lovely tune is simple to learn because of the repetition of the soprano and alto lines. Meter changes ($\frac{6}{8}$, $\frac{9}{8}$, and $\frac{6}{8}$), chromatic movement during the modulation, musical phrasing, and dynamic contrasts make this song a valuable teaching addition to the repertoire.
Level of difficulty: Beginning; for very young choirs

Composer: Kirkpatrick, Ralph; arr. David Willcocks
Title: Away in a Manger (from *Carols for Choirs I,* fifty Christmas carols edited and arranged by Reginald Jacques and David Willcocks)
Publisher: Oxford University Press
Voicing: Unison children's choir, mixed choir or piano accompaniment
Style: English folk (seasonal)
Language: English
Notes: This is a lovely SATB arrangement of "Away in a Manger" that works beautifully with the children singing the soprano line and the piano playing all four voices. Children can also sing the soprano line while an adult choir hums the other three voices. This setting is in F major, in three strophic verses, with a melodic range from C_4 to D_5.
Pedagogical value: In learning this piece, children need to work on producing long, open vowel sounds to sustain a beautiful legato. The choir must also learn to finish each phrase before starting the following phrase.
Level of difficulty: Beginning; for very young choirs

Composer: Klouse, Andrea
Title: John Henry: The Real Story
Publisher: Hal Leonard #08599363
Voicing: Two parts, unaccompanied
Style: American folk (spiritual)
Language: English
Notes: This piece is a popular arrangement of the lively American folk song "John Henry" and the great spiritual "This Train." Both tunes are appealing to young students. The form is strophic with a slow introduction and verse. There is a spoken narration at the beginning.
Pedagogical value: These melodies offer an excellent opportunity to introduce young singers to blue notes found in jazz. The arrangement presents opportunities to develop independence of parts against simple harmony. A discussion about the origins of folk songs and spirituals and how they are part of our musical heritage will help put these two pieces into a broader perspective. To perform in authentic style, "smears" or portamentos and a train whistle are appropriate. Simple choreography created by the students would also be effective.
Level of difficulty: Intermediate

Composer: Kodály, Zoltán
Title: Ave Maria
Publisher: Universal Edition; Theodore Presser 312-40592
Voicing: Three parts, unaccompanied
Style: Contemporary
Language: Latin
Notes: This Ave Maria is a three-part, antiphonal setting. It is arranged in such a way that each line of the chant is introduced by a solo section and followed by a refrain. In this setting, Kodály introduces an archaic antiphonal structure found in some liturgies.
Pedagogical value: This is a valuable composition for the more advanced choir. Latin vowel pronunciation and correct breath control should be emphasized.
Level of difficulty: Advanced

Composer: Kodály, Zoltán
Title: Cease Your Bitter Weeping
Publisher: Boosey and Hawkes #1890
Voicing: Three parts, unaccompanied
Style: Contemporary
Language: English
Notes: This is an example of choral ostinato with variation. The piece begins with octave unison singing by the alto and the first sopranos; the remainder of this work is in three or more parts.
Pedagogical value: This unaccompanied choral contains advanced harmonies and will challenge most young choirs. The meter changes provide opportunities to explore and experience constantly changing movement.
Level of difficulty: Advanced

Composer: Kodály, Zoltán
Title: Christmas Dance of the Shepherds
Publisher: Theodore Presser #212-40573
Voicing: Two parts, unaccompanied (optional piccolo)
Style: Contemporary (seasonal)
Language: English
Notes: This two-part folk song, homophonically arranged with a rhythmic ostinato, is an excellent character piece. The folklike style is enhanced by piccolo obbligato.
Pedagogical value: This folk carol is an excellent tool for introducing the ostinato. Unaccompanied singing of this kind develops vocal independence.
Level of difficulty: Intermediate

Composer: Kodály, Zoltán
Title: Ladybird
Publisher: Boosey and Hawkes #5674
Voicing: Three parts, unaccompanied
Style: Hungarian folk
Language: English
Notes: Based on a Hungarian children's folk song, this work contains an ostinato with a descant in the top voice. Although the harmony is static, the piece generates much of its excitement from an intense rhythmic drive. "Ladybird" employs the Hungarian "snap" rhythm so often found in the music of Brahms and Liszt.
Pedagogical value: English diction, introduction of a rhythmic ostinato, and independence of line are all reasons to include this tune in a young choir's choral library.
Level of difficulty: Intermediate

Composer: Kodály, Zoltán, arr.

Title: 'Mid the Oak Trees

Publisher: Boosey and Hawkes #20095

Voicing: Three parts, unaccompanied

Style: Hungarian folk

Language: English

Notes: This folk song is a three-part setting that is basically an unaccompanied modern adaptation of imitative techniques used in pre-Baroque, unaccompanied choral music.

Pedagogical value: " 'Mid the Oak Trees" introduces the young singer to the modal, melodic character of Hungarian folk music. Unaccompanied singing requires careful listening and exact intonation, and the "snap" rhythm of the piece is exciting as well as educational for the choir.

Level of difficulty: Advanced

Composer: Kurth, Burton

Title: A Cookie for Snip

Publisher: Leslie Music Supply no. 1049 (Canada)

Voicing: Unison, piano accompaniment

Style: Contemporary

Language: English

Notes: The text for this piece is by Margaret Hutchison. It is in D major, in $\frac{4}{4}$ time, with a range from D_4 to D_5.

Pedagogical value: This short, very easy song sits nicely, moving constantly through the octave range. The melody is made up of four different phrases in ABA form. The three-bar B phrase climbs with the help of G♯; the climbing describes the urgency of the child convincing the listener that his dog should have a cookie too. A staccato ending (three notes) to one phrase gives an opportunity to contrast staccato and legato singing.

Level of difficulty: Beginning; for very young choirs

Composer: Kurth, Burton
Title: Little Boy Blue
Publisher: Leslie Music Supply no. 1089 (Canada)
Voicing: Unison, piano accompaniment
Style: Contemporary
Language: English
Notes: This piece is in E♭ major, in $\frac{6}{8}$, with a range from C_4 to E♭ $_5$. This is a nontraditional setting of the traditional nursery rhyme with an addition to the traditional text.
Pedagogical value: Though the song is very short, the youngest children will find learning the melodic line fairly challenging. Another challenge will lie in staying in tune and keeping good head tone on the low phrase "under the haystack, fast asleep" (C_4 to E♭ $_4$). The held note on "horn" may merit a little discussion on sustaining tones on open vowels.
Level of difficulty: Beginning; for very young choirs

Composer: Kurth, Burton
Title: Robin's Breakfast
Publisher: Leslie Music Supply no. 1060 (Canada)
Voicing: Unison, piano accompaniment
Style: Contemporary
Language: English
Notes: The text to this piece is written by Margaret Hutchison. It is in A♭ major, in $\frac{4}{4}$, and has a range from C_4 to E♭ $_5$. This is a short, through-composed, programmatic description of a robin catching a worm.
Pedagogical value: Rests in the melody describe the robin listening, and slurred notes describe the wiggling of the worm. Slight variations between endings of similar phrases will be a minor challenge for the youngest children.
Level of difficulty: Beginning; for very young choirs

Composer: Leslie, Kenneth; arr. Stuart Calvert

Title: Cape Breton Lullaby

Publisher: Gordon V. Thompson Music G-327

Voicing: Three parts, piano accompaniment

Style: Canadian folk

Language: English

Notes: This homophonic folk arrangement is particularly beautiful and worth careful attention. Centering around the key of E♭, the step-wise voice leading is logical and easy to sing. The four-bar phrases are similarly voiced, making learning short and easy. The second section contrasts in tessitura, key, and dynamic. The verses contrast with solo and humming chorus returning to the final statement, which is reminiscent of the opening section. The piano accompaniment doubles the melody and offers an expressive and supportive arpeggiation. The edition includes a pronunciation guide to some of the geographic locations mentioned in the text.

Pedagogical value: The study and performance of this Canadian folk-song arrangement can teach young choristers to appreciate the many unique aspects of Canadian culture. Particularly characteristic of Canada's Eastern Provincial folk songs, melodies from Cape Breton are unusually beautiful and seem to characterize the people of this island, who cherish their culture.

Level of difficulty: Intermediate

Composer: Lotti, Antonio

Title: Miserere Mei

Publisher: Boosey & Hawkes #5232

Voicing: Three parts, unaccompanied

Style: Baroque

Language: Latin

Notes: This piece reflects the learned *prima prattica* that still prevailed in early Baroque music. The polyphonic setting uses melodic tension created by the use of suspensions (a hallmark of Lotti's style). Word painting is an important part of this particularly expressive work.

Pedagogical value: This piece requires vocal independence and harmonic awareness. The Latin diction demands carefully formed vowels and supported, legato singing.

Level of difficulty: Intermediate

Composer: Lübeck, Vincent
Title: Christmas Cantata
Publisher: Chantry Music Press
Voicing: Two parts, organ or piano accompaniment, strings or woodwinds
Style: Baroque (seasonal)
Language: English

Notes: Written for two equal voices, this mini-extended work can be studied and performed by beginning or intermediate choirs. The music begins with a short instrumental sonata, played by violins and organ (or piano) followed by five stanzas of vocal material. The texture is polyphonic, and is supported by a chordal accompaniment.

Pedagogical value: This early Baroque cantata written by the sixteenth-century Hanoverian composer Vincent Lübeck was discovered after World War II in Berlin. Lübeck was one of the great organ virtuosi of his generation, and also a great teacher. Young choirs will certainly benefit from the study and performance of this simple and expressive choral music. The two voices remain independent and easy to hear, the accompaniment provides melodic and harmonic support, and the harmonic suspensions and dotted rhythms offer young choirs the opportunity to understand some of the characteristics of Baroque style.

Level of difficulty: Intermediate

Composer: Luboff, Norman, arr.

Title: A Capital Ship

Publisher: Walton Music WW 1064

Voicing: Three parts, piano accompaniment (four hands)

Style: American folk

Language: English

Notes: Arranged by one of America's foremost choral artists and folk-song scholars, this work demonstrates the late Norman Luboff's interest in children's voices. This "sailor song" tells of adventures at sea, with a jolly captain and a mad crew who weather a storm, run ashore, have some fun, and forever pledge their lives to the sea "on a capital ship." The final refrain announces: "I'll stay no more on England's shore, so let the music play...." Luboff's arrangement is set in the key of E♭ major, modulating in the second section to F major. The rhythm is stated in simple quarter-note patterns in $\frac{4}{4}$. The texture is predominantly homophonic, and the verses are contrasted by the varying and imaginative use of *sprechstimme* (in canon), and solo verses.

Pedagogical value: The educational value of this American folk song lies in the dramatic interest of the story line as it develops, verse to verse. While the homophonic part singing will pose some challenges, the dramatic import and lighthearted character of this sailor song motivates young choirs to sing with enjoyment.

Level of difficulty: Advanced

Composer: MacCillivray, Allister; arr. Stuart Calvert
Title: Song for the Mira
Publisher: Gordon V. Thompson Music G-326
Voicing: Three parts, piano accompaniment (optional oboe or flute)
Style: Canadian folk
Language: English
Notes: In dancelike triple meter, this unforgettable melody is arranged for treble choir in six verses. In the key of D major, each verse is varied in texture and dynamic range from unison to three-part homophonic voicing. The Mira is a river in Cape Breton, Nova Scotia, an eastern province in Canada.
Pedagogical value: There is much to learn from this special Canadian folk-song arrangement, from the contrast of each verse in text, dynamic, and texture, to the cultural and aesthetic import of the expressive melody and sentimental words. The repeated syncopated rhythms offer a challenge to the singers because they vary slightly from verse to verse. Solo and small-ensemble singing help to create variation between the verses.
Level of difficulty: Intermediate

Composer: McKelvy, James, arr.
Title: Deck the Halls in $\frac{7}{8}$
Publisher: Mark Foster #MF953
Voicing: Three parts, unaccompanied
Style: Contemporary (seasonal)
Language: English
Notes: This is a spicy addition to the traditional seasonal concert. The familiar melody is accompanied by counter melodies above or below the melody and, for the second verse, modulates to the dominant.
Pedagogical value: This is an effective and appealing way for children to develop a feeling for $\frac{7}{8}$ meter and to develop an understanding of the tonic/dominant relationship.
Level of difficulty: Advanced

Composer: Mahler, Gustav
Title: Bell Chorus (from the Third Symphony)
Publisher: Edward B. Marks No. 31
Voicing: Unison children's chorus, three-part treble women's choir, piano, percussion
Style: Romantic
Language: German/English
Notes: The Bell Chorus from Mahler's Third Symphony offers a broad range of harmonic color and dynamic contrast. The unison children's choir imitates the sound of bells, singing the syllables "bimm bamm." The treble women's chorus sings homophonically, outlining the German text from Mahler's song cycle "Des Knaben Wunderhorn."
Pedagogical value: This piece offers an excellent introduction to the late Romantic style, using long phrases, dynamic contrast, and changing harmonies. The "Bell Chorus" can be used as a choir festival selection, combining high school girls choir with elementary children's choir. It can serve as an introduction to the fifth movement of Mahler's Third Symphony.
Level of difficulty: Beginning (with advanced three-part treble choir)

Composer: Martin, William, arr.
Title: Charlottown
Publisher: Lawson-Gould #51335
Voicing: Three parts, unaccompanied
Style: American folk
Language: English
Notes: This rhythmic folk song is based on a repeated pattern in duple meter. The familiar, stepwise melody is organized in four-bar phrases. Martin's arrangement uses modulation, dynamic variation, and rhythmic augmentation to contrast each setting of the melody. The choir experiences antiphonal singing, canonic entries, and homophonic sections throughout.
Pedagogical value: The rhythmic variation of this folk-song arrangement can be used to compare and contrast even and uneven time values, here manifested as eighth-note and dotted-eighth-note patterns.
Level of difficulty: Intermediate

Composer: Mason, Lowell; arr. Doreen Rao
Title: O Music
Publisher: Boosey & Hawkes #6352
Voicing: Unison, piano accompaniment; three parts, unaccompanied
Style: Classical (American school song)
Language: English
Notes: Lowell Mason, an important historical figure in American music education, wrote many songs for school music. This simple, stepwise melody in G major is organized in three four-bar phrases. The text signals the invitation "let the chorus sing." In this octavo there are two arranged versions: one for unison voices with a simple piano accompaniment, and one for unaccompanied choir in three-part canon.
Pedagogical value: A good warm-up song or opening concert piece, "O Music" celebrates singing in the choir. This song encourages the understanding of major tonality, legato phrasing, and the ability to sing parts. The text is full of pure vowels and easily vocalized consonants. Children can enjoy singing a simple melody and focus on the development of musicianship skills.
Level of difficulty: Beginning; for very young choirs

Composer: Mendelssohn-Bartholdy, Felix
Title: Ye Sons of Israel (from *Laudate pueri Dominum*)
Publisher: E. C. Schirmer #1839
Voicing: Three parts, piano accompaniment
Style: Romantic
Language: Latin/English
Notes: Mendelssohn's work in E♭ major reflects long, legato phrases characteristic of the Romantic style. The structure is essentially binary—ABAB form, alternating between contrapuntal entries on the text, "Ye sons of Israel," and homophonic entries on the text, "O Praise the Lord." The harmonic rhythm is fairly quick, with many characteristic suspensions and modulations. The work has a wide dynamic range, also characteristic of Mendelssohn's Romantic style.
Pedagogical value: In studying and performing Mendelssohn, students can compare and contrast contrapuntal and homophonic textures, major and minor tonalities, and dynamic changes characteristic of the Romantic style. The students can develop singing skills, including breath management and vowel formation, necessary to perform long phrases and dynamic changes.
Level of difficulty: Advanced

Composer: Miller, Sy and Jill Jackson
Title: Let There Be Peace on Earth
Publisher: Shawnee Press, Inc. #E-38
Voicing: Two parts, with descant, piano accompaniment
Style: Contemporary
Language: English
Notes: Ades and Hawley have arranged this contemporary song on a popular text that holds great audience appeal. Arranged in strophic form, the words suggest that "peace begins with me." The voices sing a sustained melody over the D major harmonic outline in the arpeggiated piano accompaniment. The long phrases are Romantically conceived with examples of both polyphonic and homophonic writing.
Pedagogical value: In the studying and performance of this piece, students will be able to practice the breath management necessary to achieve a legato line.
Level of difficulty: Intermediate

Composer: Mozart, Wolfgang Amadeus
Title: Ave verum corpus
Publisher: E. C. Schirmer #484
Voicing: Two parts, piano, organ, or string accompaniment
Style: Classical
Language: Latin/English
Notes: Long, sustained phrases characterize this well-known motet. The voices move homophonically in thirds and sixths. There are constant quarter notes in the piano or string part that move against the sustained vocal line, and the harmonic tension of the work's suspensions give the music a continuous pulse and legato feel.
Pedagogical value: The study and performance of this work teaches children to exercise the vocal techniques and musicianship skills necessary to perform and enjoy the "choral classics." To perform this work, students must learn to sustain four-bar phrases by practicing breath management exercises. They can learn to control the rise and fall of the melody through the open vowel sounds and supported voiced consonants like the "v" and "m" of the text "Ave verum."
Level of difficulty: Intermediate

Composer: Nelson, Havelock
Title: Stay, Little Blackbird
Publisher: Gordon V. Thompson Music G.138
Voicing: Unison, piano accompaniment
Style: Contemporary
Language: English
Notes: The text to this piece was written by Lucia Turnbull. The work is organized in two strophic verses, in G major, in $\frac{2}{2}$, with a range from C_4 to E_5. **Pedagogical value:** This is a charming short piece that does not take long to learn but provides some brief challenges in range and pitch learning. The verses each consist of five two-bar phrases. The last two phrases incorporate, as part of a harmonically interesting sequence, a lowered seventh in the melody.
Level of difficulty: Beginning; for very young choirs

Composer: Nelson, Ron
Title: Ask the Moon (No. 3 from *Three Settings of the Moon*)
Publisher: Boosey & Hawkes #6100
Voicing: Two parts, piano accompaniment (optional classroom percussion)
Style: Contemporary
Language: English
Notes: The composer sets this distinct and appealing poetry in a through-composed style with overlapping phrases. The unison melody is basically tonal with few intervallic jumps. The simple two-part texture moves in thirds and octaves; there are changes from simple to compound meter throughout. The song includes optional percussion parts that can be played on Orff instruments.
Pedagogical value: The study and performance of this piece teaches the relationship of text to melody and rhythm. The students can speak the poetry in its original literary form (printed on the inside cover) and then chant the poetry rhythmically. Word painting devices can be discovered and explored throughout the piece. The instrumental texture encourages an understanding of the potential combinations and variations of vocal and instrumental tone color.
Level of difficulty: Intermediate

Composer: Nelson, Ron
Title: Autumn Lullaby for the Moon (No. 2 from *Three Settings of the Moon)*
Publisher: Boosey & Hawkes #6099
Voicing: Two parts, piano accompaniment (optional instrumental accompaniment)
Style: Contemporary
Language: English
Notes: The slow, sustained lullaby is built on a whole-tone scale, and while the vocal range is limited, the musical effect can be hauntingly beautiful. The dynamic level stays soft, and the articulation smooth and legato throughout the piece. The Thomas Ahlburn lullaby text is depicted with sensitivity, making this work most appealing to young choirs and their audiences.
Pedagogical value: Studied in relation to the other two selections in *Three Settings of the Moon,* "Autumn Lullaby" contrasts in dynamic, rhythm, and range. This quasi-extended choral work provide the opportunity for children to understand the principles of musical contrast.
Level of difficulty: Intermediate

Composer: Nelson, Ron
Title: Four Anthems for Young Choirs
Publisher: Boosey & Hawkes #5576
Voicing: Unison, organ or piano accompaniment
Style: Contemporary
Language: English
Notes: These short Biblical texts are sensitively set with lyrical melodies. For development, the first is treated canonically before a very simple coda. Others have similar simple melodic material, using a few syncopations or accidentals to spark interest without undue complexity. Only one of the pieces is actually "unison": one is a three-part canon and the other two have short (possibly optional) "divisi" sections.
Pedagogical value: The accessible counterpoint provides children with an opportunity to develop part-singing skills. The third song begins and ends with phrases vocalized on "oh."
Level of difficulty: Beginning; for very young choirs

Composer: Nelson, Ron

Title: He Came Here for Me

Publisher: Boosey & Hawkes #5371

Voicing: Four parts, piano accompaniment

Style: Contemporary (seasonal)

Language: English

Notes: In this carol, Ron Nelson creates an ethereal setting with open chords in the accompaniment and a unison vocal introduction sung on an "o" vowel. The carol is in three parts, in ternary ABA form: the A sections are groups in two-bar phrases and simple, repetitive rhythms. The B section is marked "with great intensity." The upper and lower voices sing in octaves, outlining open chords.

Pedagogical value: The study and performance of this contemporary carol offers the choir an opportunity to practice the ensemble skills of listening and of making necessary changes and improvements in rhythm and pitch. The unison and octave singing on a neutral vowel requires exact intonation, achieved with the use of breath support and unified vowel formation throughout the ensemble.

Level of difficulty: Advanced

Composer: Nelson, Ron

Title: Miniatures from a Bestiary, Parts I and II (A Choral Cycle)

Publisher: Boosey & Hawkes #6452; 6453

Voicing: Unison to three parts, piano accompaniment (optional instrumental accompaniment)

Style: Contemporary

Language: English

Notes: This set of short, imaginative, and highly crafted songs for treble voices and piano is developed around the sound and meaning of animal poems by Kenneth Rexroth. The musical construction, based on an octatonic scale (alternating whole and half steps), varies from piece to piece according to the natural rhythm and intonation of the poems. The texts themselves, describing the Eagle, the Cat, the Goat, the Raccoon, and "I" in Part I, and the Trout, the Lion, the NIOkapi, the Deer, and the Monkey in Part II, are simple but offer opportunities for discovery and problem-solving by the choristers. The distinctive yet independent piano accompaniment establishes the tonal centers and harmonic changes, supporting the young voices throughout the work.

Pedagogical value: The study and performance of these pieces encourages the skills of good diction, careful listening, and sensitivity to dynamic change. The poetic and musical substance of the compositions offers a variety of musical challenges and artistic opportunities associated with the performance of contemporary choral music.

Level of difficulty: Intermediate

Composer: Nelson, Ron
Title: The Moon Does Not Sleep (No. 1 from *Three Settings of the Moon*)
Publisher: Boosey & Hawkes #6098
Voicing: Two parts, piano accompaniment (optional instrumental accompaniment)
Style: Contemporary
Language: English
Notes: The mood of Thomas Ahlburn's poem is depicted with long vocal phrases sustained over a shimmering and rhythmic piano accompaniment. The $\frac{6}{8}$ time fluctuates between a pulse of two and three, according to the rhythm of the text. The third section is marked "free and unmeasured," suggesting a choral recitative sung over a repeated, arpeggiated ostinato accompaniment.
Pedagogical value: This song offers the young choir an opportunity to study and perform many musical aspects of comtemporary choral technique. These include the use of changing harmony from dissonant tone clusters and intervals to consonant homophonic thirds and sixths set in traditional major-minor chord progressions. Nelson combines many different compositional ideas to convey the powerful poetry in a musical and aesthetically appealing manner.
Level of difficulty: Intermediate

Composer: Nelson, Ron
Title: Slumber Now Beloved Child (from *The Christmas Story*)
Publisher: Boosey & Hawkes #5542
Voicing: Three parts (optional piano or celesta accompaniment)
Style: Contemporary
Language: English
Notes: Set in $\frac{3}{4}$ time, this contemporary carol is a lullaby. The upper two voice parts sing in thirds over a descending, sustained line in the alto voice part. The piano accompaniment is scored completely in the treble clef, giving a high-voice color to the work.
Pedagogical value: The study and performance of this contemporary carol offers students the opportunity to develop an understanding of timbre and vocal skills associated with phrasing. Students should have the opportunity to discover the phrase structure and perform the short phrases musically.
Level of difficulty: Intermediate

Composer: Niles, John Jacob, and Lewis Henry Horton
Title: I Wonder as I Wander
Publisher: G. Schirmer #9360
Voicing: Three parts, piano accompaniment
Style: American folk (seasonal)
Language: English
Notes: This Appalachian carol is set in C natural-minor (Aeolian). The form is strophic: in this arrangement, each voice part sings one verse while the other two support it homophonically on a neutral "hum." The piano accompaniment doubles the harmony of the voices over a tonic pedal. The $\frac{6}{8}$ meter gives the familiar melody its lilting quality.
Pedagogical value: Studying and performing this popular American folk song gives young singers the opportunity to learn the musicianship skills related to singing minor modes, particularly the Aeolian mode.
Level of difficulty: Intermediate

Composer: Nordoff, Paul, arr.
Title: My Lord, What a Morning (from *Spirituals for Children to Sing and Play*)
Publisher: Theodore Presser 411-41044
Voicing: Unison, piano accompaniment
Style: American folk
Language: English
Notes: This spiritual is arranged in E major, in $\frac{4}{4}$ time, with a range from E_4 to E_5. The song is in ABA form, with a short coda. The setting is very simple, enhancing the quiet majesty of the melody.
Pedagogical value: This wonderful, sustained melody is not difficult for young children to learn. The dynamic markings are generally *mf, f,* and *ff*: they might be taken down to a comfortable level for very young voices, but this song can be beautifully sung on a young child's dynamic level.
Level of difficulty: Beginning; for very young choirs

Composer: Orrego Salas, Juan
Title: Canticos de Navidad
Publisher: Boosey & Hawkes #OC3B6489
Voicing: Three parts, unaccompanied
Style: Contemporary (seasonal)
Language: Spanish/English
Notes: This charming set of three short Christmas pieces reflects the rhythms and harmonic qualities characteristic of the composer's Latin American origins. The first piece is rather somber, the second is an exquisite "Alleluya" which could be programmed separately, and the third piece is a lively "Danza" with hand claps to accompany the triple meter.
Pedagogical value: The continuity and variety illustrated in the juxtaposition of these three selections is a lesson in musical architecture for singers of any age. In addition, each piece is rich with rhythmic, melodic, and harmonic material for children to study and perform.
Level of difficulty: Advanced

Composer: Ouchterlony, David
Title: The Gentle Donkey (from *Carol Cantata*)
Publisher: Leslie Music Supply no. HC 1014 (Canada)
Voicing: Unison, piano accompaniment
Style: Contemporary (seasonal)
Language: English
Notes: This piece is in three strophic verses in D♭ major, in $\frac{6}{8}$, with a range from D♭$_4$ to E♭$_5$. The text tells the story of the donkey carrying Mary to Bethlehem, delivering her safely, and staying by her. The song is in a rocking rhythm suggestive of the donkey's gentle walk and his unwillingness to hurry.
Pedagogical value: This song is fairly complex, melodically and textually, for very young children, but they can learn it and sing it well—and it is very appealing to them. Each verse consists of six long phrases; no two phrases are similar. It is a wonderful song to develop a long legato line with the challenge of wordy phrases.
Level of difficulty: Beginning; for very young choirs

Composer: Ouchterlony, David
Title: On the Night When Jesus Was Born
Publisher: Gordon V. Thompson Music G-157
Voicing: Unison, piano accompaniment
Style: Contemporary (seasonal)
Language: English
Notes: This piece, in three strophic verses, is in F major, in $\frac{6}{8}$ time, with a range from C_4 to D_5. The first two verses ask why the angels sang and why the wise men came on bended knee; the third verse answers that Mary knew all the while.
Pedagogical value: This song is complex melodically and textually, with long, flowing phrases. Rhythmic variations between the three verses on the third phrase need a little extra work. An additional challenge is the melodic twist in the last phrase, in which an A♭ (over a D♭ major triad in the piano) is followed by an A♮ as part of a descending F major triad—presenting a good opportunity for a discussion of flats and naturals.
Level of difficulty: Beginning; for very young choirs

Composer: Page, Nick, arr.
Title: Niska Banja (Serbian Gypsy Dance)
Publisher: Boosey & Hawkes OC4B6517
Voicing: Four parts, piano accompaniment (four hands)
Style: Yugoslavian folk
Language: Serbian
Notes: Niska Banja is a folk song/dance popular throughout Yugoslavia. To Central Europeans the $\frac{9}{8}$ rhythm of 2+2+2+3 is as natural as a $\frac{4}{4}$ rock beat is in North America. The vocal parts are arranged almost exactly as they would be in Yugoslavia, but the piano parts are quite different from those of traditional Yugoslav instruments. The driving rhythm is a characteristic feature.
Pedagogical value: Dancers would do a lively four-step dance to this song (in which the fourth step or skip is slightly longer than the others). As a rehearsal exercise, the chorus could stand on their toes and bounce their heels down on each beat, with the fourth bounce being a little longer and higher than the others. As soon as the rhythm is felt, the song becomes infectious. The editor's notes include a pronunciation guide.
Level of difficulty: Intermediate

Composer: Palestrina, Giovanni Pierluigi da
Title: Gloria Patri
Publisher: Bourne Co. ES 46A
Voicing: Three parts (two choirs), unaccompanied
Style: Renaissance
Language: Latin/English
Notes: This piece suggests a fanfare. The four-bar phrases are sung antiphonally between two choirs as statement and echo. The voicing is homophonic; each phrase ends with an imperfect cadence.
Pedagogical value: The study and performance of this work provides the opportunity for students to learn the musicianship skills associated with homophonic, antiphonal singing. Students enjoy experimenting with choir placement according to the acoustics of the performance area.
Level of difficulty: Intermediate

Composer: Parke, Dorothy
Title: The Ferryman
Publisher: Gordon V. Thompson Music G-143
Voicing: Unison, piano accompaniment
Style: English
Language: Contemporary
Notes: This text is by Christina Rosetti. The piece is in E major, in $\frac{4}{4}$ time, with a range from E_4 to E_5. The short, easy melody flows nicely in quarter notes over steady eighths in the accompaniment.
Pedagogical value: The melody consists of two phrases repeated in rondo form, in a conversation between a ferryman and his passenger. This could be done antiphonally by children in two groups, or with a solo ferryman.
Level of difficulty: Beginning; for very young chorus

Composer: Parke, Dorothy

Title: Who's That a-Knocking?

Publisher: Gordon V. Thompson Music G-143

Voicing: Unison, piano accompaniment

Style: Contemporary

Language: English

Notes: The text of this song is by Emile Jacot. The piece is in E minor, in $\frac{2}{4}$ time, with a range from E_4 to E_5.

Pedagogical value: This is a nice companion piece to the Ferryman, with which it is published. It is also very short and easy. There are brief opportunities for special articulation on the words "one knock, two knocks" (tenuto followed by staccato on successive quarter notes) and for the exercise of crescendos and decrescendos.

Level of difficulty: Beginning; for very young choirs

Composer: Persichetti, Vincent

Title: sam was a man

Publisher: G. Schirmer #9791

Voicing: Two parts, piano accompaniment

Style: Contemporary

Language: English

Notes: Through the canonic use of e. e. cummings' poetry, Persichetti musically portrays a colorful image of "sam," the poem's main character. The two-part chorus is fast and intensely rhythmic. Following the unison introduction, the voice parts separate, and Persichetti uses syncopation, angular intervals, and rhythmic augmentation to depict the story. The piano adds another musical dimension, using open fifths in the bass. The canonic return of the opening melody concludes the piece.

Pedagogical value: This rhythmic, occasionally dissonant piece offers students an opportunity to develop musicianship skills related to the singing of syncopated rhythms and angular intervals. The contemporary musical material requires purposeful breath preparation and precise consonant articulation. Children's choirs enjoy the challenge and excitement of this imaginative and engaging work.

Level of difficulty: Intermediate

Composer: Peterson, Oscar
Title: Hymn to Freedom
Publisher: Walton Music, WW1135
Voicing: Three parts, piano accompaniment (optional jazz combo)
Style: Contemporary (jazz)
Language: English
Notes: This jazz ballad combines a heartfelt text about liberty with a lyrical C . major melody. The treble-voice arrangement builds chordally to a rousing cadence. The text, printed on the inside cover of the edition, can be read and enjoyed by the choir, then discussed in relation to the three-part form.

Pedagogical value: This festival piece for treble choirs is an excellent introduction to jazz ballad singing. Students can practice singing swing eighth-notes (described in the editor's notes). Choristers will learn to sing lyrically and with correct intonation, particularly in descending melodic passages where flatting can easily occur. This jazz choral appeals to young singers and audiences alike.

Level of difficulty: Intermediate

Composer: Pinkham, Daniel
Title: Angels Are Everywhere
Publisher: E. C. Schirmer #02215
Voicing: Three parts, unison, and two parts; piano accompaniment
Style: Contemporary
Language: English
Notes: This contemporary American choral cycle is made up of six individual pieces based on one unifying theme: the angel. The clever and appealing poetry is written by the composer. The pieces have a rhythmic character, and the voice parts develop homophonically. The piano accompaniment is imaginative and autonomous, but remains very supportive of the voice leadings and harmonic progressions in the chorus parts. The work was commissioned in 1987 by the American Boychoir, the Glen Ellyn Children's Chorus, and the Phoenix Boy Choir under the Consortium Commissioning Program of the National Endowment for the Arts. Each piece has separate pleasures and individual challenges.

Pedagogical value: All six pieces encourage the vocal techniques and musicianship skills required in three-part choral singing. The study of these pieces can center on text meaning in relation to the musical qualities of rhythm, tempo, harmony, and dynamics. Each piece has a contrasting character ranging from the idea of the contemporary angel in everyday life to depiction of the angel in biblical stories of old. Children enjoy practicing the simple chord changes, the major and minor scales that shape the melodic patterns, and the expressive dynamics and phrasing as they are used to contrast each of the six pieces.

Level of difficulty: Advanced

Composer: Pinkham, Daniel
Title: Ave Maria
Publisher: Associated Music Publishers #A367
Voicing: Two parts, unaccompanied
Style: Contemporary
Language: Latin
Notes: In his neo-Renaissance setting of Ave Maria, Pinkham punctuates long melismatic phrases with open cadences sustained on the open fourth or fifth. The two independent voice parts develop in chantlike style over changing meters. Changing tonal centers and independent melodic development sometimes suggest a temporarily dissonant, almost medieval quality. A supportive, resonant acoustic is preferable for the performance of this piece.
Pedagogical value: This piece illustrates the eclectic nature of contemporary American choral music. While notated in traditional, bar-lined meter, the development of the voice parts strongly suggests a nonmeasured, nonmetrical quality characteristic of early vocal music. The Latin text and the slow legato line make this an ideal opportunity to teach the vocal skills and good diction skills associated with proper intonation. The open fourths and fifths created by the independent voice parts are heard easily by young voices, but they require vocal support through the skills of breath management.
Level of difficulty: Advanced

Composer: Pinkham, Daniel
Title: Evergreen
Publisher: E. C. Schirmer #2962
Voicing: Unison, organ or piano and percussion accompaniment
Style: Contemporary
Language: English
Notes: A seamless, unison melody is sung over a four-bar chordal, piano ostinato; the melodic motion is mostly stepwise. The performance of this traditional song in a nontraditional setting illustrates the relationship of contemporary composition with early music as well as avant-garde techniques.
Pedagogical value: This piece illustrates the use of ostinato patterns. Students can explore the complete musical texture and study the relationship of the unison melody against the instrumental accompaniment. The ostinato patterns can be compared and contrasted with other examples of ostinato patterns in Baroque and jazz styles.
Level of difficulty: Beginning

Composer: Poston, Elizabeth, arr.

Title: Dance to Your Daddie (arr.)

Publisher: Boosey & Hawkes #6115

Voicing: Two parts, piano accompaniment

Style: Scottish folk

Language: English

Notes: The lilting, dancelike arrangement of this Scottish folk song is built around a four-bar melody in triple meter. Both voice parts repeat the same material as the melody alternates between them in continuous rhythmic drive. Each voice, when not singing the four-bar melody, sings a complementary countermelody supported by the piano accompaniment.

Pedagogical value: The study and performance of this tasteful and dancelike arrangement offers students an opportunity to develop the musicianship skills associated with triple meter, octave intervals, major tonality, descending melodic patterns, part singing, and vocal diction. The simple two-part form (with a fanfare coda) makes it possible for young choristers to learn the structure of the piece and memorize the music without much difficulty.

Level of difficulty: Intermediate

Composer: Praetorius, Michael; arr. Doreen Rao

Title: How Brightly Shines the Morning Star (Wie shöne leuchtet der Morgenstern)

Publisher: Boosey & Hawkes #OC2B6419

Voicing: Two parts, unaccompanied

Style: Renaissance

Language: German/English

Notes: This is one of the many contrapuntal settings of chorale tunes by the Renaissance composer Michael Praetorius. These works provide a nice relief from accompanied, unison, or homophonic choral fare.

Pedagogical value: Through the study and performance of this work, choirs can be introduced to the techniques of simple variation and counterpoint as they sing and discover how the familiar melody is varied and elaborated in the two voices.

Level of difficulty: Intermediate

Composer: Praetorius, Michael; arr. Doreen Rao
Title: Jubilate Deo
Publisher: Boosey & Hawkes #6350
Voicing: Unison canon, unaccompanied
Style: Renaissance
Language: Latin
Notes: This popular canon is ideally suited for vocal warm-ups or for a concert opening. The three-part melody covers a broad vocal range, working the head voice down into the lower singing range. When the melody is performed in three-part canon, several harmonic colors can be explored, from the dissonance of seconds to the consonance of a C major triad. The simple Latin text is sustained on pure vowels that are easily produced by the young singer.
Pedagogical value: The repeated text, "Jubilate Deo, Alleluia," offers young students the opportunity to sustain head-voice production throughout the high, middle, and lower ranges. The celebrative text encourages the idea of rejoicing and thanksgiving. The editor's notes offer a musical analysis and instructional model.
Level of difficulty: Beginning; for very young choirs

Composer: Praetorius, Michael
Title: Lo, How a Rose E'er Blooming
Publisher: G. Schirmer #10216
Voicing: Two parts, piano or organ accompaniment
Style: Renaissance (seasonal)
Language: English
Notes: This piece is a chorale. The two voice parts move homophonically with the piano supporting the voices in sustained, legato phrases. While the melody is in the soprano, the alto part adds suspensions and important modulating tones.
Pedagogical value: The long lines of this well-known music require that young students practice the skills of good breath management and vocal tone. The vowel colors should be unified between the two voice parts to assure good intonation and an even vocal blend.
Level of difficulty: Intermediate

Composer: Praetorius, Michael
Title: Psallite
Publisher: Bourne ES21A
Voicing: Three parts (optional piano accompaniment)
Style: Renaissance
Language: Latin, German, and English
Notes: This declamatory choral work is antiphonal, in ABA form. The A section has constant eighth notes patterns in all three parts, while the B section, sung in German or English, has a legato, sustained character.
Pedagogical value: This piece performs well as an opening fanfare. The antiphonal singing and dynamic contrasts of this piece invite musical experimentation in the form of alterations in the size of the ensemble, choir placement activities, and dynamic variations. The two languages (Latin and German or Latin and English) offer students practice in the diction skills associated with singing in different languages. The homophonic structure of the work invites practice in singing chord progressions on time and in tune.
Level of difficulty: Intermediate

Composer: Purcell, Henry
Title: Shepherd, Shepherd, Leave Decoying (from *King Arthur*)
Publisher: Belwin Mills #64042
Voicing: Three parts, piano accompaniment
Style: Baroque
Language: English
Notes: This two-part chorus has a predominantly homophonic texture that moves in thirds and sixths. The lilting duple meter organizes an essentially chordal, early Baroque harmony that is distributed evenly between the three voice parts. The simplicity of the part writing can be deceptive because of the tonal consonance and characteristic similarity between voice parts.
Pedagogical value: The study and performance of this chorus offers students the opportunity to develop the skills and understanding associated with singing chordal harmony in Baroque style. The students can practice the simple harmonic progressions on neutral syllables, then add text and sing rhythmically and in tempo. This harmonically simple style offers a good lesson in homophonic singing and Baroque performance practice.
Level of difficulty: Intermediate

Composer: Purcell, Henry
Title: Sound the Trumpet (from the birthday ode *Come Ye Sons of Art*)
Publisher: Lawson-Gould #787
Voicing: Two parts, piano accompaniment
Style: Baroque
Language: English
Notes: The famous two-part chorus "Sound the Trumpet" is suitable for most festive occasions or concert openings. The chorus is structured in two sections: the voices enter contrapuntally, then sing together in thirds. The phrases alternate between long, melismatic passages and short declamatory sections. The first entrance, sustained for two measures over a pedal point, is imitated by the lower voice. The B section contrasts with rapid, melismatic and rhythmically active material.

Pedagogical value: The study and performance of this chorus can be used to teach young students the ensemble skills of listening, vocal blend, and rhythmic articulation. Students should be encouraged to adjust the dynamic of their voice part to accommodate the entrance of a new subject. This work also presents an opportunity to develop the vocal skills associated with rhythmic, melismatic vocal lines.

Level of difficulty: Intermediate

Composer: Raminsh, Imant

Title: Daybreak Song (No. 4 from *Songs of the Lights*)

Publisher: Boosey & Hawkes #OC3B6273

Voicing: Three parts, piano accompaniment (orchestra parts available)

Style: Contemporary

Language: English

Notes: Based on a Navajo text, this song is introduced on a quietly assertive, unaccompanied unison, which divides in contrary motion and finally cadences on a clear open fourth. A three-part divisi section then follows with a hauntingly melodic interlude, sung softly and cadencing on a subdued D major. After a dramatic contrapuntal section, a quote from the opening chorus of the first movement of the song set, "Song of Star," returns.

Pedagogical value: In this composition, choristers can develop the musicianship skills required to perform rhythmically challenging and harmonically rich musical material. The major and minor harmonies, diverse rhythmic patterns, and wide dynamic range offer young singers many challenges—along with an equal dose of satisfaction. The tessitura requires that the children use their singing voice and support the tone with good posture and breath management. The edition includes an analysis of the work as well as teaching suggestions.

Level of difficulty: Advanced

Composer: Raminsh, Imant
Title: Song of the Stars (No. 1 from *Songs of the Lights*)
Publisher: Boosey & Hawkes #6270
Voicing: Two parts, piano accompaniment (orchestra parts available)
Style: Contemporary
Language: English
Notes: The repeated rhythmic patterns and changing meters create a chant effect characteristic of Native American verse. The musical setting of an Algonquin Indian text captures the essence of Native American ways. The vocal lines are melodic and expressive, carrying the poignant text in strong unisons and octaves. The cadences rest in minor keys, with the exception of the uniquely beautiful final D major chord. The poetry and the music are ideally interwoven by this gifted Canadian composer. Children's choirs everywhere respond to this piece with great enthusiasm.

Pedagogical value: Through the study of this text (printed on the inside cover of the choral edition), young choristers can discover both the rhythmic qualities and the formal structure of this contemporary choral composition. The changing meter can be approached through the use of movement, clapping, and chanting. The tessitura requires that the children use their singing voices and support the tone with careful breath preparation. The melodically characteristic descending fourths should be prepared during the warm-up and ear training segments of rehearsals. The edition includes an analysis of the work and teaching suggestions.

Level of difficulty: Advanced

Composer: Raminsh, Imant

Title: The Sower (No. 2 from *Songs of the Lights*)

Publisher: Boosey & Hawkes #OC3B6271

Voicing: Three parts, piano accompaniment (orchestra parts available)

Style: Contemporary

Language: English

Notes: Based on a Navajo Indian text, this piece is developed from the opening solo call: "I hold pollen of dawn in my hand..." The chorus responds with the same chantlike motive, extended and developed by the soprano and alto voices. While a rhythmic figure repeats similarly throughout the piece, the meter changes from $\frac{4}{4}$ to $\frac{3}{4}$ to $\frac{2}{4}$ in order to maintain a simple and sustained chant quality in the melody.

Pedagogical value: This song offers young choirs the opportunity to understand call-and-response singing. All voices can sing the motive, then trace its repetition through the work. This process will result in a better grasp of the form, which develops directly from the text. The tessitura requires the use of singing voice and consciously prepared breath support. The edition includes an analysis of the work as well as teaching suggestions.

Level of difficulty: Advanced

Composer: Raminsh, Imant

Title: The Sun Is a Luminous Shield (No. 3 from *Songs of the Lights*)

Publisher: Boosey & Hawkes #OC3B6272

Voicing: Three parts, piano accompaniment (orchestra parts available)

Style: Contemporary

Language: English

Notes: This piece unfolds from an expressive Native American chant, which the composer sets in a steady $\frac{9}{8}$, marked allegro ma non troppo. The imitative, linear composition is based on a major scale pattern that is developed in parallel and contrary motion. Harmonies are often dissonant—the tension of a major second is used repeatedly. The tempo alteration between the A and B sections is particularly effective in establishing the expressive import of the text.

Pedagogical value: In the study and performance of this work, students can consider the relationship of the text to the elements of the music. How the composer manipulated the elements of rhythm, melody, harmony, tempo, and dynamics in setting this particular text is directly related to the rhythm and intonation of the Native American chant. The tessitura requires that children use their singing voices and carefully support the tone with good breath preparation. The edition includes an analysis of the work as well as teaching suggestions.

Level of difficulty: Advanced

Composer: Rao, Doreen, arr.

Title: Hashivenu

Publisher: Boosey & Hawkes #OC3B6430

Voicing: Unison, canon (optional piano accompaniment)

Style: Israeli folk

Language: Hebrew

Notes: "Hashivenu" is a melodic and hauntingly memorable Hebrew song based on the Old Testament text from Lamentations: "Cause us to return Lord, to You and we shall return. Renew our days of Old." The sound and meaning of the text is fundamental to the expressiveness of the song. The rise and fall of the compound-meter melody is enhanced by the vowel and consonant qualities of the text. The long and short rhythmic values are sustained and articulated by voiced consonants and pure vowels. The editor's notes include a diction guide.

Pedagogical value: This edition offers two separate arrangements of the song: an accompanied, unison melody, and an unaccompanied canon. The two versions offer young choirs the opportunity to approach part singing from the singing of accompanied unison and the singing of unaccompanied canon. As the students feel vocally secure on the melody line, they will be ready to sing in parts.

Level of difficulty: Beginning; for very young choirs

Composer: Richardson, Michael, arr.

Title: A Hundred Pipers

Publisher: Boosey & Hawkes OCTB6511

Voicing: Three parts, piano accompaniment (optional field drum)

Style: Scottish folk

Language: English

Notes: This well-known Scottish folk song presents the image of a Scottish pipe band in formal Scottish dress: tartans, kilts, and all. Arranged in four verses, the folk song paints the picture of a hundred pipers who marched and fought against the English, staying brave and continuing to play their pipes in the face of all dangers. Their piping and their bravery dumbfounded their adversaries. Set in F major, the verses contrast with the use of unison, two-part and three-part singing in varying dynamics and rhythms. The field drum enters on the fourth verse, and an accelerando signals a fanfare coda.

Pedagogical value: With a Scottish flair, this folk song arrangement gives young choirs the opportunity to develop the skills and knowledge required in singing three-part music. The drama of the text is clearly present in the arrangement and serves as a motivation for the challenge of learning this piece. The alto voice part in the refrain lies low in the treble voice range and requires secure vocal technique.

Level of difficulty: Advanced

Composer: Richardson, Michael, arr.

Title: Promised Land

Publisher: Mark Foster Music MF 811

Voicing: Two parts, piano accompaniment

Style: American folk

Language: English

Notes: Adapted from the *Original Sacred Harp* version, Richardson's arrangement maintains much of the character and charm of early Sacred Harp singing. In the key of F minor, and in a homophonic style, the song begins with a chordal introduction to the first verse. The even, elegant rhythms of the verses are punctuated by syncopated rhythms in the refrain. The text meaning centers on the idea of the "glory of the promised land."

Pedagogical value: As part of the early American singing tradition, this Sacred Harp tune offers an opportunity to study and perform music central to the American musical heritage. The voice parts are melodically independent, assuring rapid success in part singing. The rhythmic patterns repeat and make guided sight-reading experience possible.

Level of difficulty: Intermediate

Composer: Rowley, Alec

Title: Suo-Gan

Publisher: Boosey & Hawkes #5449

Voicing: Unison, piano accompaniment

Style: Welsh folk

Language: Welsh/English

Notes: The familiar and melodious lullaby Suo-Gan has two identical verses; each verse consists of four five-bar phrases. The repeated rhythm pattern (dotted quarter note–eighth note against eighth note–dotted quarter note) is set over a straight quarter note piano accompaniment giving the lullaby a comfortably repetitive, lilting quality.

Pedagogical value: The study and performance of this familiar lullaby offers students the opportunity to develop skills required for singing long phrases composed of uneven rhythms. The dotted rhythmic figures require the ability to maintain an inner pulse and to sustain the pitch in legato style.

Level of difficulty: Beginning; for very young choirs

Composer: Runyan, Michael K.

Title: Pine Grove (from *Songs of Awakening*)

Publisher: Boosey & Hawkes OCT6561

Voicing: Three parts, piano accompaniment (orchestra parts available)

Style: Contemporary

Language: English

Notes: Published in the *Children's Choirs in Concert* series, this music can be sung by an average chorus if the vocal challenges can be met. The work is set in the Dorian mode on G, giving it an unusual tonal color. The first section is sung in unison, except for some occasional thirds. The three-part section is completely imitative. The text was written by Sara E. Sanderson.

Pedagogical value: The study and performance of this contemporary work offers young singers the opportunity to develop the vocal and musicianship skills required to perform rhythmically conceived, intervallically challenging, and melodically expressive choral music. The work should be taught in unison at a slow tempo, familiarizing all singers with the poetic ideas as they are developed musically. As students work to achieve rhythm and pitch accuracy, they will learn to appreciate the beauty of this exceptional composition.

Level of difficulty: Advanced

Composer: Runyan, Michael K.

Title: Shade of Night (from *Songs of Awakening*)

Publisher: Boosey & Hawkes OCT6562

Voicing: Three parts, piano accompaniment (orchestra parts available)

Style: Contemporary

Language: English

Notes: Published in the *Children's Choirs in Concert* series, this song portrays night as seen by a child. As the evening settles in, the child begins to fear the loneliness of the night. The tension builds and the child begins to see things in the dark, until there comes a cry of "Kyrie eleison!" The cry is repeated again and again until the child, comforted, falls asleep. The music uses recurrent themes that are easily recognizable: it begins with a theme resembling a music box and a theme of comfort. The work features antiphonal singing.

Pedagogical value: This music offers a unique opportunity to explore the subject of fear with children and introduce the Mass text "Kyrie eleison" in a non-liturgical setting. The final melody is perhaps one of the most beautiful in all of today's children's choir repertoire.

Level of difficulty: Advanced

Composer: Runyan, Michael K.

Title: Wings of Morning (from *Songs of Awakening*)

Publisher: Boosey & Hawkes OCT6603

Voicing: Three parts, piano accompaniment (orchestra parts available)

Style: Contemporary

Language: English

Notes: Published in the *Children's Choirs in Concert* series, this song begins with a depiction of the earliest sounds of the morning as nature is just beginning to awaken; the voices imitate the soft, brittle sounds of early dawn. In the next section, the piece begins to develop the sensation of flight with a lofty unison melody over even eighth notes. The music develops imitatively on a text inspired by Psalm 139:9.

Pedagogical value: The study and performance of this contemporary work will offer young singers the opportunity to develop the vocal and musicianship skills required for singing dissonant intervals, dynamic variations, and legato lines, and for imitative part singing. The predominantly tonal composition lends itself to the use of simple solfège exercises.

Level of difficulty: Advanced

Composer: Rutter, John

Title: Donkey Carol

Publisher: Oxford University Press #82-111

Voicing: Two parts, piano accompaniment (optional chamber orchestra)

Style: Contemporary (seasonal)

Language: English

Notes: The $\frac{5}{8}$ meter defines the character of this piece, portraying the uneven gait of a donkey's walk. The vocal form is strophic: Rutter differentiates between verses with unison singing, simple harmony, canon, and melody with descant. The third bar of each four-bar phrase has five eighth notes, creating momentum toward the following phrase.

Pedagogical value: The study and performance of this piece can introduce students to the musicianship skills associated with singing uneven duple meter in $\frac{5}{8}$. The consistent four-bar phrasing offers a musical constant to set off the uneven meter. The development of skills associated with singing uneven meter is made easier and more enjoyable through the use of body movement and conducting activities.

Level of difficulty: Beginning; for very young choirs

Composer: Rutter, John
Title: For the Beauty of the Earth
Publisher: Hinshaw Music #HMC-469
Voicing: Two parts, piano accompaniment (small orchestra optional)
Style: Contemporary
Language: English
Notes: This composition is based on poetry by F.S. Pierpoint set to a flowing, diatonic melody placed over a simple harmonic outline (given in the piano accompaniment). The rhythm alternates between sustained whole notes, eighth notes, and ornamented quarter notes. Rhythmic syncopation is used in the voice parts and the piano material. The first verse is sung in unison, an alto part is added in the second verse, and a descant is added in the third verse.
Pedagogical value: The study and performance of this popular work requires the use of supported head voice and careful diction. Students should be encouraged to sing in a light, legato manner without forcing or pushing the voice into a heavy chest mechanism—particularly in the lower parts of the vocal range where flatting is most likely to occur.
Level of difficulty: Beginning; for very young choirs

Composer: Rutter, John
Title: Jesus Child
Publisher: Oxford University Press #U156
Voicing: Unison, piano accompaniment
Style: Contemporary (seasonal)
Language: English
Notes: In this seasonal work (appropriate in some settings for use in a holiday program), Rutter uses staccato articulation, accents, and syncopation to give the music its catchy rhythmic flavor. The use of subito dynamic changes and a legato dolce section add contrast and keep the young singers' interest.
Pedagogical value: The study and performance of this work offers students the opportunity to practice the vocal skills required to sing in a legato, yet syncopated style. Students should be taught to sing lightly in the "singing voice" (head voice mechanism) and avoid the speaking voice (chest voice mechanism) that interrupts the possibility for good intonation and legato performance.
Level of difficulty: Beginning; for very young choirs

Composer: Rutter, John
Title: Nativity Carol
Publisher: Oxford University Press #U154
Voicing: Unison, piano accompaniment (optional recorder and percussion)
Style: Contemporary (seasonal)
Language: English
Notes: "Nativity Carol" has a lilting, rhythmic character. It is composed in strophic form: each verse begins with a simple three-bar phrase.
Pedagogical value: The study and performance of this contemporary carol requires sustained, legato singing over three-measure phrases. By comparing and contrasting verses, the students can be led to the discovery of this simple vocal form. The optional instrumental ensemble adds variety to the texture and interest to the study and performance of this popular contemporary work.
Level of difficulty: Beginning; for very young choirs

Composer: Rutter, John
Title: Shepherd's Pipe Carol
Publisher: Oxford University Press #U141
Voicing: Unison, piano accompaniment
Style: Contemporary (seasonal)
Language: English
Notes: This carol is light and rhythmic. The meter fluctuates from simple to compound; the voice parts outline chordal patterns, alternating between legato and staccato articulations. The composer has added syncopation and surprise modulations to keep interest.
Pedagogical value: The study and performance of this contemporary carol offers young singers the opportunity to develop the musicianship skills required to perform mixed meters. The contrast between simple meter and compound meter can be mastered through movement activities, conducting exercises, and clapping and chanting activities. This kind of practice will ensure expressive and accurate performance.
Level of difficulty: Intermediate

Composer: Saint-Saëns, Camille
Title: Praise Ye the Lord (from *Christmas Oratorio*)
Publisher: Boosey & Hawkes #5285
Voicing: Two parts, piano or organ accompaniment
Style: Romantic
Language: Latin/English
Notes: The melody in this piece consists of the elegant lyrical phrases typical of French Romantic composition. The rise and fall of the melody is closely united with the meaning of the text; dynamics are used to shape the phrases. The second section moves harmonically in thirds and in contrary motion. The vocal parts are doubled in the keyboard accompaniment.
Pedagogical value: The stepwise melody and simple rhythms are easily accessible to young singers, making this a good piece to begin studying in the fall for the holiday concert. The Latin text promotes the development of uniformly shaped vowels.
Level of difficulty: Intermediate

Composer: Salieri, Antonio; arr. Gordon Binkerd
Title: Chimes
Publisher: Boosey & Hawkes #6224
Voicing: Two parts, bell lyra
Style: Contemporary
Language: English
Notes: This piece by Mozart's famous contemporary consists of a simple melody, sung in canon. The text portrays a dinner bell, a door bell, and a church bell. The melody is extended and embellished by a variety of bell-like vocal effects. The bell lyra (or other bell-like instrument) provides a sparse accompaniment in addition to taking a turn at the canon melody.
Pedagogical value: The melodic line allows young singers the use of their full vocal range. The structure of this piece provides young singers with the opportunity to experience textural variety: at times they sing unaccompanied, at times they sing with a second vocal part imitating bells, and finally they engage in two-part singing with the instrument. Vocal warm-ups that develop forward resonance will help the students sing the bell sounds in tune.
Level of difficulty: Intermediate

Composer: Schein, Johann
Title: Kikkehihi
Publisher: Boosey & Hawkes #6103
Voicing: Three parts, unaccompanied
Style: Renaissance
Language: German/English
Notes: This piece is typical of the late Renaissance Italian madrigal, which borrowed scenes from pastoral poetry. The text is about a hen and a rooster greeting the morning ("Kikkehihi" is the German equivalent of the sound of the hen). The translator for this edition notes that while the piece may sound complex on first hearing, a close examination reveals its simplicity. The polyphonic writing offers each voice a line to shape and to embellish contrapuntally.
Pedagogical value: This madrigal, in AB form, motivates students to discover and practice melodic sequences in the contrasting B section. The stepwise motion of the melody contributes to the accessibility of the piece for young singers.
Level of difficulty: Intermediate

Composer: Schein, Johann; arr. Victoria Glaser
Title: O Lovely Child (O schönestes Kindelein)
Publisher: E. C. Schirmer #2519
Voicing: Two parts, piano or organ accompaniment
Style: Baroque
Language: English
Notes: This motetlike piece opens with an ascending phrase in imitation and ends with an ascending line treated in a similar manner. The AABB form remains polyphonic throughout the work except for one brief homophonic segment. Organ is used as the accompanying instrument, but the piano can be substituted effectively. In the accompaniment, the left hand provides a continuo-style bass line while the right hand often doubles the vocal line.
Pedagogical value: The equal voice parts are imitative in this polyphonic piece. Young singers will enjoy discovering the techniques of contrapuntal writing, including imitation, sequences, and suspensions. The edition features extensive dynamic markings, which will help students shape the musical phrases.
Level of difficulty: Intermediate

Composer: Schubert, Franz
Title: Fischerweise (Fisherman's Song)
Publisher: Gordon V. Thompson Music #G-193
Voicing: Unison, piano accompaniment
Style: Romantic
Language: German
Notes: This edition offers both German and English text, encouraging young singers to discover how the musical material mirrors the text—a practice typical of this genre. The vocal line is primarily conjunct in nature and lies in a very suitable range (D_4 to E_5). The melodic outline is chordal in nature, relating closely to the harmonic structure of the piece. The arpeggiated piano accompaniment reflects the mood and character of the fisherman's boat rolling on the sea.
Pedagogical value: This is an especially good piece with which to introduce young singers to German *lieder*. The challenge of this Romantic style is to maintain the sense of legato singing and to avoid choppiness despite the quick melodic rhythm.
Level of difficulty: Beginning; for very young choirs

Composer: Schubert, Franz
Title: Peace (Pax vobiscum)
Publisher: E. C. Schirmer #1078
Voicing: Unison, piano accompaniment
Style: Romantic
Language: English
Notes: This piece reveals Schubert's supreme gifts for crafting beautiful melodies in even the simplest of songs. The serenity of the text is mirrored in the flowing legato phrases and soft dynamics. The chordal piano accompaniment duplicates the melodic rhythm and doubles the vocal line throughout most of the song.
Pedagogical value: The tessitura of the melody lies in the middle of young singers' vocal range, making this an accessible piece for beginning choirs. Students will experience the shaping of phrase through dynamic variation. Young singers will surely respond to the beauty of this art song from the Romantic period.
Level of difficulty: Beginning; for very young choirs

Composer: Schubert, Franz
Title: Sanctus (from the *German Mass*)
Publisher: Plymouth Music Company
Voicing: Three parts, piano accompaniment
Style: Romantic
Language: English/German
Notes: This piece is a lovely, short choral with two strophic verses. The melody is in the top voice, and the texture of the vocal lines as well as the keyboard accompaniment is homophonic.
Pedagogical value: This is a wonderful piece for young students to experience three-part singing. The tempo is quite slow, and each vocal line moves primarily in a stepwise motion. Students have the opportunity to practice part-singing in tune in a chordal context.
Level of difficulty: Advanced

Composer: Schubert, Franz
Title: To Music (An die Musik)
Publisher: Boosey & Hawkes #6366
Voicing: Unison, piano accompaniment
Style: Romantic
Language: English/German
Notes: This vocal classic is an example of the close union between music and poetry characteristic of Romantic style. The text, which conveys the power of music to change life, is expressed in the lyrical rise and fall of legato, four-bar phrases. The contrasting piano accompaniment is a steady eighth-note figure around which the melody is interwoven in the treble and bass lines. The form—introduction, verse one, interlude, verse two, coda—is similar to other vocal compositions of the period.
Pedagogical value: This piece, so dependent on beautiful phrasing, will provide young singers the opportunity to practice breath control for long phrases, to learn to sustain the forward movement of a phrase, and to determine how dynamic changes shape melodic phrases.
Level of difficulty: Intermediate

Composer: Schultz, Donna Gartman
Title: Orkney Lullaby
Publisher: Boosey & Hawkes #6469
Voicing: Two parts, piano accompaniment (also arranged in three parts)
Style: Contemporary
Language: English
Notes: This folklike music will immediately appeal to young choirs. Sung by the sopranos, the melody captures the expressiveness of the text ("Orkney," in the title, refers to an island off the coast of England.) The alto part, which moves in contrary motion, has its own wonderful melodic characteristics. The arpeggiated piano accompaniment provides the rocking motion of this lullaby and supports the harmonic structure of the vocal parts.
Pedagogical value: Discovering the form of the piece—A (E minor), B (B minor), A (E minor)—and the modulation between parts A and B enhances the students' understanding of this music. The phrase structure is irregular, and the six-bar phrases require good breath support to sustain them musically.
Level of difficulty: Intermediate

Composer: Schumann, Robert
Title: Autumn Song (Herbstlied)
Publisher: Fostco Music Press #MF 858
Voicing: Two parts, piano accompaniment
Style: Romantic
Language: English/German
Notes: This piece, which is about the change that takes place in autumn, is a fine example of the expressive, well-crafted melodies of the Romantic period. The alto line is of equal importance to the soprano melody and lies in a suitable range. The form of the song is AABB coda. The piano accompaniment is quite rhythmic and supportive of the vocal lines in the A section; in contrast, it contains an arpeggiated figure in the B section.
Pedagogical value: The challenge in this piece is presented in the interesting rhythm of the melody. This is especially true of the rhythmic interplay of parts when the text calls for birds to "sing."
Level of difficulty: Intermediate

Composer: Schumann, Robert
Title: Were I a Tiny Bird
Publisher: Fostco Music Press #MF854
Voicing: Two parts, piano accompaniment
Style: Romantic
Language: German/English
Notes: The text of this German *lied* is mirrored in the warm and expressive musical phrasing. The long, archlike melody characterizes the vocal writing of the Romantic period. The piano accompaniment enhances and supports the vocal line. This homophonic song is in ABA form, and the range is well suited for young singers.
Pedagogical value: The flowing legato phrases provide young singers with the opportunity to practice the principles of legato articulation, including forming uniform vowels free of diphthongs, singing through to the ends of words, and ending phrases together. Additionally, attention should be given to using dynamics to shape the musical phrase.
Level of difficulty: Intermediate

Composer: Schütz, Heinrich; arr. Don McAfee
Title: Lord, Create in Me a Clean Heart (Schaffe in mir, Gott, ein reines Herz)
Publisher: Belwin-MIlls #DMC 8091
Voicing: Two parts, piano accompaniment
Style: Baroque
Language: German/English
Notes: This is one of several motets from the collection "Kleine geistliche Konzerte" (Little Sacred Concertos) written by this early Baroque composer. It is scored for one to five solo voices and continuo. The piece begins with two equal voice parts alternating musical phrases either in direct imitation or with pitch and rhythmic variation. Rhythmic interest and contrast is provided through the use of hemiola and a short, melismatic ending.
Pedagogical value: The melody moves primarily in a stepwise motion and contains no difficult intervals or large leaps. The work lies comfortably within the students' vocal range. Young singers will experience the rhythmic challenges posed in this polyphonic composition through the use of suspensions, three-against-two rhythms, and an ending melisma.
Level of difficulty: Advanced

Composer: Shaw, Geoffrey, arr.
Title: The Golden Vanity
Publisher: E. C. Schirmer #1805
Voicing: Unison with descant, piano accompaniment
Style: English folk
Language: English
Notes: Young singers are drawn to the text of this haunting song about a young man who saves the ship "The Golden Vanity" and then is denied his reward. A descant, sung with three of eight verses in this strophic song, adds musical variety and expands the harmonic texture. The predominantly chordal piano accompaniment often doubles the vocal parts.
Pedagogical value: The rousing quality of this song depends on rhythmic accuracy in singing the melody. Students can practice rhythms by singing the pattern of an eighth note followed by a sixteenth note, which occurs frequently in the first phrase of the verses. The tessitura of the primarily conjunct melody lies in the upper-middle range and is quite suitable for young singers.
Level of difficulty: Intermediate

Composer: Sibelius, Jean; arr. Gwynn S. Bement
Title: For Thee, Suomi (Excerpt from *Finlandia*)
Publisher: E. C. Schirmer #1855
Voicing: Two parts, piano accompaniment
Style: Romantic
Language: English
Notes: The arrangement of this well-known song is derived from the melodic and harmonic material of the orchestral tone-poem *Finlandia*. The lyrical music translates effectively to the vocal medium, and though text is an added element, it reflects the composer's love for his country and nature. The song is sometimes used in Finland as a national anthem.
Pedagogical value: Dynamics are very important in the expressiveness of this song. Observing and practicing the expressive markings that shape the phrases contributes to an effective performance.
Level of difficulty: Intermediate

112

Composer: Simeone, Davis, and Onorati
Title: The Little Drummer Boy
Publisher: Shawnee Press Inc. #B-180
Voicing: Two or four parts, piano accompaniment
Style: Contemporary (seasonal)
Language: English
Notes: This charming piece has been a favorite seasonal selection of choral singers of all ages. The octavo is scored for SA or SSAA: the top two voices carry the melody with harmony, and the bottom two voices produce the "prum-pum" sound of the drum. Both the melody and harmony remain the same throughout all the three verses. The piano accompaniment provides a drumlike cadence on chords in the left hand.
Pedagogical value: Young singers can discover the melodic sequences in the third phrase of the verses. The chordal harmony is challenging and requires practice to sing in tune.
Level of difficulty: Intermediate

Composer: Sleeth, Natalie
Title: O Come, O Come Immanuel
Publisher: Choristers Guild #CGA-273
Voicing: Unison with descant, piano accompaniment
Style: Contemporary (seasonal)
Language: English
Notes: Natalie Sleeth's lyrical composition presents a melody and text different from the traditional song with the same title. The legato phrases are beautifully written in primarily stepwise motion. Following a short, contrasting middle section, the opening melody returns embellished—this time by a soaring and complementary descant. The range and melodic quality of this octavo is ideally suited for the young choir.
Pedagogical value: The legato phrases encourage the use of controlled breathing to sustain support through the last note of a phrase; the melodic rhythm includes several dotted half notes and whole notes. Singing the long notes of this piece, students learn to master open vowel sounds free of diphthongs. The range of the descant promotes the use of the students' higher and lighter singing voice. The highest pitches occur at the crest of an ascending phrase and on words with open vowels to encourage the best singing.
Level of difficulty: Beginning; for very young choirs

Composer: Smith, Gregg, arr.
Title: The Cuckoo
Publisher: G. Schirmer #11695
Voicing: Two parts, piano accompaniment
Style: American folk
Language: English
Notes: Based on a collection of American folk songs by John Jacob Niles, this pentatonic song is organized in strophic form with an ending coda. The first two verses are sung by soloist or chorus in unison, the third verse is arranged with a humming alto part, and the altos sing the melody while the sopranos sing an upper part in the fourth verse. The text of this hauntingly beautiful song centers on the typical early-American folk theme of damsels and false-hearted lovers. A guitar-style piano accompaniment adds even more folklike character to the piece.
Pedagogical value: This piece provides an opportunity for students to sight-read a pentatonic song in the minor mode. The melodic intervals are quite simple for young singers—though the choristers will be challenged by the inclusion of wider intervals of sixths and sevenths.
Level of difficulty: Intermediate

Composer: Sowerby, Leo, arr.
Title: The Snow Lay on the Ground
Publisher: H. W. Gray Publications #GCMR 2822
Voicing: Three parts, piano accompaniment
Style: American folk (seasonal)
Language: English/Latin
Notes: This lovely seasonal carol combines both English and Latin texts. The Latin "Venite adoremus Dominum" is given an unusual setting in a cheerful rhythmic $\frac{6}{8}$. The carol is homophonic, in four verses; a descant using the Latin text is added in the second and fourth verses.
Pedagogical value: The wide range in this song encourages the development of vocal control in both the upper and lower ranges. Vocal preparation can focus on singing the pitches in the high range with a free, floating quality and bringing that lightness into the lower pitches.
Level of difficulty: Intermediate

Composer: Specht, Judy, arr.

Title: The Saucy Sailor

Publisher: Gordon V. Thompson Music #G-237

Voicing: Unison (occasional divisi), piano accompaniment

Style: Canadian folk

Language: English

Notes: The text of this novelty piece is about a sailor, John, who wants to marry Nancy, who only loves John's money. Each character is represented by its own tonality—John by E♭ major and Nancy by E major—and their music is sung in unison by the chorus. The chorus then divides into two, three, and sometimes four parts to comment briefly (with "yes" and "no") on the progress of the relationship. The piano accompaniment is sparse and doubles the vocal line.

Pedagogical value: The rhythms, melodic intervals, and part writing are all quite easy. The melody for John consists primarily of intervals within the pentatonic scale, making at least a portion of this song excellent material for sight-reading.

Level of difficulty: Beginning; for very young choirs

Composer: Sprenkle, Elam

Title: For a Dewdrop (from *A Midge of Gold*)

Publisher: Boosey & Hawkes #6496

Voicing: Unison, piano accompaniment

Style: Contemporary

Language: English

Notes: This lovely song is one of eleven from the cycle *A Midge of Gold* commissioned for the tenth anniversary of the Children's Chorus of Maryland. Based on a poem by Eleanor Farjeon, the music reflects the text in a manner similar to songs from the Romantic period. The role of the piano accompaniment is also similar to that of the Romantic style; it conveys the mood and character of the piece.

Pedagogical value: This piece gives young singers the opportunity to master the challenging intervals in the contour of this melody. They will discover how the composer's score markings contribute to the expressiveness of this very delicate song.

Level of difficulty: Intermediate

Composer: Sprenkle, Elam
Title: October's Party (from *A Midge of Gold*)
Publisher: Boosey & Hawkes #6495
Voicing: Two parts, piano accompaniment
Style: Contemporary
Language: English
Notes: Young singers will respond enthusiastically to the delightful text about dressed-up and dancing trees. Each of the vocal parts is a singable melody, and the rhythms are irresistibly dancelike. The vocal range of the song is C_4 to E_5. The homophonic piano accompaniment supports the vocal lines with some altered rhythms that provide an interesting contrast.
Pedagogical value: The pattern of a dotted eighth followed by a sixteenth and the syncopated eighth-quarter-eighth note pattern figure prominently in the melodic rhythm of this song. Here young singers can practice and perform these patterns with precision. The vocal writing promotes the use of the higher and lighter range of the young singing voice. The phrases, including the highest pitches, should be practiced first on an open neutral syllable such as "bah," to ensure a relaxed, open vocal production.
Level of difficulty: Intermediate

Composer: Starer, Robert
Title: Midnight
Publisher: Canyon Press Juilliard Repertory Library, Vol. I
Voicing: Two parts, piano accompaniment
Style: Contemporary
Language: English
Notes: The text of this song is filled with silly contradictions that appeal to the young singer's sense of humor. The work begins in unison and changes to a two-part canon. Each part sings different words from the unison section. The sparse piano accompaniment and modal setting contribute to the rather haunting character of this piece.
Pedagogical value: The expressive qualities of dynamic and tempo changes lend excitement to this song. Young students discover how the composer's notations in the score provide the directions for these changes.
Level of difficulty: Beginning

Composer: Stone, David
Title: Space Travellers
Publisher: Boosey & Hawkes #6116
Voicing: Unison, piano accompaniment
Style: Contemporary
Language: English
Notes: The colorful text, a poem comparing a witch to a futuristic character from outer space, will delight children's love of fantasy. The melodic phrases are quite short and rhythmic, requiring excellent diction for a successful performance. The steady walking bass line in the piano accompaniment provides a contrast to the more rhythmic quality of the melody.
Pedagogical value: Though the melody uses primarily conjunct motion, it includes the intervals of a fourth, a fifth, and an octave which will challenge young choirs to sing in tune. Students experience how sharp contrasts in dynamics contribute to the expressiveness of the song.
Level of difficulty: Beginning; for very young choirs

Composer: Strauss, Johann; arr. Lavater
Title: Tales from the Vienna Woods
Publisher: Lawson-Gould #51361
Voicing: Two parts, piano accompaniment
Style: Romantic
Language: English
Notes: Music written for instrumental ensembles does not generally translate well to the vocal medium, but this arrangement of the well-known waltz is effective and will delight singers and audiences alike. The text provided is suitably matched to the melody, and humming and "la" passages contribute to the joyful expressiveness of the song. The piano accompaniment frequently doubles the vocal lines and provides the waltz rhythm throughout.
Pedagogical value: The rhythmic nature of this piece gives young singers a chance to practice and perform correctly the relationship of the quarter note and quarter rest, the eighth note and eighth rest, and the dotted quarter and dotted half notes. The extensive score markings (for example, those for first and second endings), *dal segno* repeats, and directions to go *al fine* and to the coda will improve students' ability to read the musical score.
Level of difficulty: Intermediate

Composer: Strommen, Carl, arr.

Title: Dream Angus

Publisher: Boosey & Hawkes #6233

Voicing: Three parts, piano accompaniment

Style: Scottish folk

Language: English

Notes: The arrangement of this lovely Scottish lullaby is for three parts, but the two verses are sung in unison and only the refrain is in three-part harmony. The tessitura is in the middle to lower part of the students' singing range, and each of the vocal lines moves predictably within the harmonic structure. The piano accompaniment throughout the verses is a rocking eighth-note pattern that contrasts with the legato vocal line of the lullaby text.

Pedagogical value: The simple rhythms and primarily scalar movement of the melody make this a good piece for sight-reading. The part writing in the refrain will encourage students to listen to the chordal harmonies and to sing them in tune.

Level of difficulty: Intermediate

Composer: Sweelinck, Jan Pieterszoon; arr. Doreen Rao

Title: Vanitas, vanitatum (Vanity, Vanity, All Is Vanity)

Publisher: Boosey & Hawkes #6351

Voicing: Four parts, unaccompanied

Style: Renaissance

Language: Latin

Notes: When sung as a four-part canon, this piece by the late Renaissance Netherlands composer has a beautiful motetlike sonority achieved through the use of the sustained dotted rhythm in the opening phrase and a more melismatic second phrase. An effective performance of this piece might include positioning four sections of the chorus in different parts of the room to enhance the polyphonic texture and to duplicate performance practices of the period. The edition includes a pronunciation guide to the simple Latin text.

Pedagogical value: The unison canon melody provides an opportunity for the chorus to practice uniform vowel sounds, articulated consonants, and complete musical phrases before moving on to the greater challenge of part singing. Because the Latin text contains pure vowel sounds, this song promotes the development of uniformly shaped vowels.

Level of difficulty: Intermediate

Composer: Tallis, Thomas; arr. Douglas E. Wagner
Title: The Tallis Canon
Publisher: Somerset Press #MW 1230
Voicing: Two to four parts, piano accompaniment
Style: Renaissance
Language: English
Notes: The arranger has altered the melody of this well-known English Renaissance canon and provided two additional verses. It is easy for young singers because of the stepwise movement and simple rhythms. The piano accompaniment, consisting primarily of running eighth notes, provides a rhythmic contrast to the more legato melody line.
Pedagogical value: This is a good piece with which to introduce students to polyphonic singing. The simple melody will promote security in unison singing and enable choristers to maintain their part against two or three other vocal lines.
Level of difficulty: Beginning

Composer: Thiman, Eric H.
Title: I Have Twelve Oxen
Publisher: Novello #SMR 441
Voicing: Two-part canon, piano accompaniment
Style: Contemporary
Language: English
Notes: The melody is the same for each verse (except for the last measure of the third verse). It is written in canon; the two voice parts take turns being the leader. The range, F_4 to E_5 (with one high F), promotes the use of the head voice mechanism. The piano accompaniment is chordal and provides harmonic support for the vocal lines.
Pedagogical value: The melody is primarily stepwise, making this a good piece to use for sight-reading. Students will discover the *fa*-sharp (*fi*), which occurs very prominently in the last phrase of the first two verses.
Level of difficulty: Beginning; for very young choirs

Composer: Thiman, Eric H., arr.
Title: Kitty of Coleraine
Publisher: Boosey & Hawkes #6138
Voicing: Unison with descant, piano accompaniment
Style: Irish folk
Language: English
Notes: The two verses of this song appeal to the child's sense of humor. The words describe a rather unusual courtship. The phrase structure for each verse is A A' B A" (based on the Irish folk idiom). A descant in the second verse provides contrast and accentuates the drama of the story. The rhythm, an easy duple ($\frac{6}{8}$), is based on eighth notes and uses occasional dotted eighths and sixteenths. This rhythm enhances the lilting, dancelike quality of the melody.

Pedagogical value: This song allows young singers to work on several familiar tonal patterns that appear in the melodic phrases. These include *so–mi–do, do–mi–so,* and *so,–la,–ti,–do.* Because of the rhythmic nature of the melody, care needs to be taken to sing the four-bar melodic phrases with a flowing, forward movement.

Level of difficulty: Beginning; for very young choirs

Composer: Thiman, Eric H.
Title: The Path to the Moon
Publisher: Boosey & Hawkes #6114
Voicing: Unison, piano accompaniment
Style: Contemporary
Language: English
Notes: This song is a wonderful example of the artistic use of text to shape the melodic phrases. The picturesque words, which describe a longing "to sail the path to the moon" are mirrored in the upward movement of the melodic line. The tessitura lies in the middle to upper part of the singers' range, so it requires vocal preparation. The musical satisfaction derived from singing this beautiful song will justify the effort.

Pedagogical value: The song provides singers with the opportunity to develop a sense of musical phrasing. Attention should be paid to the rise and fall of the phrases and to the difference in their length. Because several of the phrases start on Eb $_5$, the singers will need to learn to breathe for the open vowel, support the tone, and sing with a relaxed, open throat.

Level of difficulty: Beginning; for very young choirs

Composer: Thiman, Eric H.
Title: When Cats Run Home
Publisher: Boosey & Hawkes #5570
Voicing: Two parts, piano accompaniment
Style: Contemporary
Language: English
Notes: The staccato nature of this charming two-part song enhances the "misterioso" text by Alfred Lord Tennyson. It is set in canon, with each voice part getting a chance to be the leader. The minor tonality and the dramatic character of the accompaniment contribute to a sense of suspended animation.
Pedagogical value: The canonic form provides an opportunity for young singers to experience polyphonic singing in a musical setting more elaborate than a simple round. The text is quite descriptive. Careful attention must be paid to dynamics and expressive markings for an effective performance.
Level of difficulty: Beginning; for very young choirs

Composer: Thompson, Randall
Title: The Place of the Blest
Publisher: E. C. Schirmer #2800, #2801 & #2839
Voicing: Three parts, piano accompaniment (orchestra parts available)
Style: Contemporary
Language: English
Notes: An American choral classic for young treble voices, "The Place of the Blest" was first performed in 1969. The sustained melodies, long legato phrases, and predominantly homophonic part writing do a good job of conveying the appealing poetry by Robert Herrick. The music represents some of Randall Thompson's best work. Children respond with enthusiasm and commitment to the complex, yet relevant poetic texts: "The Carol of the Rose," "The Pelican," "The Place of the Blest," and "Alleluia." Performed with piano or chamber orchestra, these four movements can be programmed individually or as part of an extended work. The three-part voicing develops melodically and can be successfully performed by choirs that work on a regular basis.
Pedagogical value: The pedagogical value of studying and performing Randall Thompson's choral music lies in the opportunity to sing the music of one of America's most celebrated choral composers. The melodic quality and sensitive poetry combine to make an educationally valuable and publicly appealing performance experience.
Level of difficulty: Advanced

Composer: Thompson, Randall
Title: Velvet Shoes
Publisher: E. C. Schirmer #2526
Voicing: Two parts, piano accompaniment
Style: Contemporary
Language: English
Notes: The image of velvet shoes in this simple and beautiful song evokes the tranquillity of a walk in the snow. The legato nature of the melodic phrasing reflects the peaceful mood of the text, while the bass line in the piano accompaniment provides a marchlike contrast. The form, A (sung by the sopranos), B (sung by the altos), A (sung by sopranos and altos in unison), and coda (a simple two-part phrase), makes this a very suitable song for young singers.
Pedagogical value: The stepwise movement of this melody and the simple melodic rhythm make this a good song for sight-reading. Breathing exercises should be included in warm-ups to help the students sustain breath support through the four-bar phrases.
Level of difficulty: Intermediate

Composer: Thomson, Virgil, arr.
Title: My Shepherd Will Supply My Need
Publisher: H. W. Gray #GCMR 2562
Voicing: Two parts, piano accompaniment
Style: American folk (hymn)
Language: English
Notes: This is a wonderful piece with which to introduce young singers to the Southern American folk hymn. The pentatonic melody in each of the three verses of this strophic song is organized in an AABA phrase structure. The third phrase presents a vocal challenge because of the high F's and G's. While the homophonic setting of the alto part and accompaniment remain the same, variety is achieved among the three verses through contrasts in dynamics.
Pedagogical value: The rhythms and the A phrases of the melody are all easily accessible to young singers. Because of the high tessitura of the third phrase, however, vocal warm-ups must be practiced before attempting to sing this work without strain. These exercises could be vocalises that promote a relaxed, open throat.
Level of difficulty: Intermediate

Composer: Tidball, Norman
Title: Boots and Saddles
Publisher: Boosey & Hawkes #6118
Voicing: Two parts, piano accompaniment
Style: Contemporary
Language: English
Notes: The melody of this cheerful piece is quite accessible to beginning choral singers. There are no difficult leaps and the melodic rhythms are simple. Except for a few low A's and B♭'s, the tessitura is in the middle to upper range of the young voice. There is a brief section in harmony, but generally the alto part is characteristic of a countermelody. The piano accompaniment, as might be expected from the title, consists primarily of a "trotting" rhythm. This song would be appropriate for the lighter section of a choral concert.
Pedagogical value: Young singers enjoy discovering the form of this piece: A (sung in unison), A' (in two parts), B, A, and coda. They also become aware of the use of accidentals used extensively in the B section.
Level of difficulty: Beginning; for very young choirs

Composer: Track, Gerhardt, arr.
Title: Come Now and Gather (Ihr Kinderlein kommt)
Publisher: G.I.A. Publications #G-2159
Voicing: Two parts, piano accompaniment
Style: German folk
Language: German/English
Notes: The arrangement of this gentle lullaby includes both the German and the English texts. The texture of the three verses moves from unison, to two-part, to imitative, to solo with humming accompaniment. Though the range is quite suitable for young singers, the humming accompaniment in the alto part is in the lower part of their range and must be sung lightly. The piano accompaniment doubles the vocal lines in all three verses, adding variety with the rise of arpeggiated chords in the third verse.
Pedagogical value: The humming line for the third verse moves primarily downward in thirds. The challenge for young singers is to keep the stepwise intervals in tune by paying close attention to the placement of the whole and half steps.
Level of difficulty: Intermediate

Composer: Track, Gerhardt, arr.

Title: Rejoice and Be Glad (Oh Jubel, oh Freud)

Publisher: G.I.A. Publications #G-2154

Voicing: Two parts, piano accompaniment

Style: German folk

Language: German/English

Notes: Each of the three verses in this carol from the Austrian province of Carinthia has two sections that are arranged differently, providing rhythmic and melodic contrast. Sopranos and altos take turns singing the melody while the added part is often an "Ah" or humming descant. Both the English and the German texts are printed in the score, but this is truly more beautiful when sung in the German.

Pedagogical value: The melody consists primarily of eighth notes and is rhythmic in nature. Young singers will experience the challenge of articulating the eighth notes within the context of a legato melodic line.

Level of difficulty: Intermediate

Composer: Vaughan Williams, Ralph

Title: Children's Christmas Song (from *Folk Songs of the Four Seasons*)

Publisher: Oxford University Press

Voicing: Two parts, piano accompaniment

Style: English folk (seasonal)

Language: English

Notes: This delightful song is from Part IV, Winter, of the *Four Seasons* set and is based on the traditional carol "Here We Come A-Wassailing." Contrast in the melody line is provided through the use of changing meter: One $\frac{6}{8}$ section is rhythmic and bouncy, and another is more legato, moving from $\frac{2}{4}$ to $\frac{3}{4}$ and back. The first, second, and fifth verses are homophonic. In the third and fourth verses, the altos sing the rhythmic melody while the sopranos provide a legato descant.

Pedagogical value: In the third and fourth verses, the young singers will experience three against two rhythms: the altos sing the more rhythmic melody with a pulse of three while the sopranos sing a legato descant in duple meter. In the homophonic verses, the challenge is to sing accurately the long and short of the quarter-note, eighth-note rhythm pattern.

Level of difficulty: Intermediate

Composer: Vaughan Williams, Ralph
Title: An Invitation (from *Children's Songs*)
Publisher: Oxford University Press #55.017
Voicing: Unison, piano accompaniment
Style: Contemporary
Language: English
Notes: The invitation in the text is for "poor fellows" who live in the town to come to the country for freedom and happiness. There are frequent meter and key changes, which effectively mirror the words of the text. This piece was composed for an English children's choir and is a wonderful example of this composer's gift for writing music that is appealing to young singers.
Pedagogical value: The meter changes frequently from $\frac{6}{8}$ to $\frac{9}{8}$. Here, students can practice the melodic rhythm, feeling the change from duple to triple meter while the eighth-note pulse remains constant. The melody is primarily conjunct, and the challenge is to correctly sing the larger intervals within the tonality of each successive key.
Level of difficulty: Intermediate

Composer: Vaughan Williams, Ralph
Title: Land of Our Birth (from *Song of Thanksgiving*)
Publisher: Oxford University Press #54.226
Voicing: Unison (optional descant, piano or organ accompaniment)
Style: English folk (patriotic)
Language: English
Notes: This stirring song, based on a text by Rudyard Kipling, presents a patriotic message similar to that of "God Our Fathers" and "America." The vocal range of the melody, which remains the same for the four verses, is D_4 to D_5. After a modulating interlude from B♭ major to D major (between the verses and the coda), the range expands to include a few high F's and one high G, which occur in ascending passages. The thick texture of the homophonic piano accompaniment promotes the feeling of strength and pride expressed in the text.
Pedagogical value: Young singers will experience the change in accent as the meter alternates between $\frac{4}{4}$ and $\frac{5}{4}$ in the verses. Additionally, the tessitura of the descant in the fourth verse and in the coda will offer students the opportunity to learn to sing higher pitches without strain and with correct intonation.
Level of difficulty: Intermediate

Composer: Vaughan Williams, Ralph, arr.
Title: Linden Lea
Publisher: Boosey & Hawkes #219
Voicing: Three parts, piano accompaniment
Style: English folk
Language: English
Notes: This piece, scored in this arrangement for three parts, was originally a solo song. The setting of the vocal lines alternates between homophonic and polyphonic texture. The text, melody, and harmonies—all folklike in character—reflect the composer's love for his native England.
Pedagogical value: The melody lies in the soprano part and is the same for all three verses. The phrase structure for the melody is AABBA; students will discover where the phrases are the same and where they differ. Communication of this song depends on good choral diction, and young singers can practice and perform crisp articulation of the consonants and singing on open vowels.
Level of difficulty: Advanced

Composer: Vaughan Williams, Ralph
Title: Orpheus with His Lute
Publisher: Oxford University Press #OCS52
Voicing: Unison, piano accompaniment
Style: Contemporary
Language: English
Notes: The text for this graceful unison song is a poem by William Shakespeare paying homage to Orpheus the musician. The music is through-composed, with flowing legato phrases of unequal length. The vocal range, D_4 to E_5, is perfectly suited for the treble voice. Though the piano accompaniment does not double the vocal line, it provides harmonic support and textural interest.
Pedagogical value: Well-formed, focused vowels and well-articulated consonants contribute to the legato phrasing necessary in a successful performance of this song. An additional challenge for young singers is to learn to shape the melodic phrases through the use of dynamics.
Level of difficulty: Beginning; for very young choirs

Composer: Vaughan Williams, Ralph
Title: Prologue (to the Ploughboy) (from *Folk Songs of the Four Seasons*)
Publisher: Oxford University Press #54.264
Voicing: Unison with two-part descant, piano accompaniment (orchestra parts available)
Style: English folk
Language: English
Notes: This exhilarating song is the Prologue of the Cantata. The charming text is of a time gone by when ploughboys earned their living reaping and mowing the grain. The melody, which is sung by a unison chorus, remains the same throughout all three verses and is varied through the use of dynamics. The two-part, smaller chorus adds a descant with the joyful words, "let's sing and be merry," to verses two and three. This song is a wonderful piece to open a concert.
Pedagogical value: Young singers can discover the way the composer both repeats and varies the several melodic sequences in this piece. In addition, students' ability to read the musical score will aid the descant chorus in getting their pitches from the melody sung by the unison chorus.
Level of difficulty: Intermediate

Composer: Vaughan Williams, Ralph
Title: She's Like the Swallow
Publisher: Oxford University Press
Voicing: Unison, piano accompaniment
Style: Canadian folk
Language: English
Notes: This folk song from Newfoundland is a lovely piece in the Dorian mode. The melody contains intervals of a fourth and fifth, which are well placed within the harmonic structure. The four phrases are in the shape of an arc: the beginning pitches of the first two phrases get successively higher and the beginning pitches of the last two phrases successively lower. The piano accompaniment provides some rhythmic and melodic contrast.
Pedagogical value: Young singers will discover that the only accidental in the melody is the sharped *fa* (*fi*) characteristic of the Dorian mode. Because the rhythm of the melodic phrases is quite simple, this is a good piece for students to sight-read.
Level of difficulty: Beginning; for very young choirs

Composer: Vaughan Williams, Ralph
Title: Spring (from *Three Children's Songs*)
Publisher: Oxford University Press #55.015
Voicing: Unison, piano accompaniment
Style: Contemporary
Language: English

Notes: This is the first in a collection of three songs dedicated to a British children's chorus. The text describes various characteristics of each of the four seasons. "Smiling spring," the poet's favorite, is saved for last. The melody and accompaniment change slightly for each season, reflecting the mood; for example, the mode shifts to the minor for winter. The reflective character of this graceful song appeals to young singers.

Pedagogical value: The tonality of this through-composed song changes frequently, providing the challenge of learning melodic intervals within the context of brief new tonal centers. This can be accomplished with solfège.

Level of difficulty: Intermediate

Composer: Vaughan Williams, Ralph
Title: Two Songs of Winter (from *Folk Songs of the Four Seasons*)
Publisher: Oxford University Press #54.263
Voicing: Unison with descant, piano accompaniment
Style: English folk
Language: English

Notes: These two songs from the winter section of Vaughan Williams's cantata are contrasted in tonality, tempo, and mood, and work well together. "God Bless the Master," from the "Sussex Mummers Carol," consists of three verses set in strophic form and includes a lovely optional descant to be sung with the last phrase of the third verse. Harmonic and rhythmic changes and a thickening texture in the piano accompaniment, plus a gradual growth in dynamics, contribute to the building intensity of this dramatic song. The rhythmic "Wassail Song" is performed at a more lively tempo. A descant is added to the fifth and sixth verses, providing textural and harmonic interest to this song.

Pedagogical value: The legato phrasing in "God Bless the Master" requires correct breathing technique to sustain support for the full length of the legato phrases and to produce the increase in dynamics. The melismatic passages in the descant of "Wassail Song" promote the development of vocal flexibility as students learn to control the eighth-note patterns.

Level of difficulty: Intermediate

Composer: Vivaldi, Antonio; arr. Dennis Martens
Title: Gloria in excelsis (from *Gloria*)
Publisher: Walton Music Corp.
Voicing: Three parts, piano accompaniment
Style: Baroque
Language: Latin/English
Notes: This is a treble-voice arrangement of the opening Gloria from Vivaldi's well-known composition. The melodic line alternates between short rhythmic motives and longer legato phrases. The primarily homophonic texture of the vocal lines is contrasted with a very rhythmic contrapuntal piano accompaniment.
Pedagogical value: In the more rhythmic section of this piece, young singers will gain control of the pattern of a dotted eighth followed by a sixteenth note. The legato section challenges the students to maintain breath support and energy through the long whole-note phrases.
Level of difficulty: Advanced

Composer: Vivaldi, Antonio; arr. Dennis Martens
Title: Laudamus Te (from *Gloria*)
Publisher: Walton Music #W5014
Voicing: Two parts, piano
Style: Baroque
Language: Latin/English
Notes: The "Laudamus Te," a duet, is the third movement of Vivaldi's *Gloria*, a Baroque classic. The texture alternates between contrapuntal and homophonic passages. The text, which is printed in both English and Latin in this edition, is cheerful and uplifting. Vivaldi wrote the *Gloria* while in the employment of a girls' orphanage, and his ability to write music that suits young voices is beautifully present here.
Pedagogical value: In this song, the students will experience two-part singing in a contrapuntal texture. The Latin text promotes uniform vowel formation because Latin has more open vowel sounds and fewer diphthongs than many other languages.
Level of difficulty: Advanced

Composer: Walters, Edmund
Title: The Cuckoo Carol
Publisher: Boosey & Hawkes #5721
Voicing: Two parts, piano accompaniment
Style: Contemporary (seasonal)
Language: English
Notes: The delightful text of the unison carol in this arrangement is about a cuckoo, a dove, and a pigeon (each with their own call) visiting the manger at Bethlehem. Written in mixed meter ($\frac{6}{8}$ and $\frac{9}{8}$), the melody is the same for each of the three verses with the rests in the melody expanding each time after the bird calls. The piano accompaniment, a reduction of an orchestral arrangement, provides a wonderful contrast to the simple melody.
Pedagogical value: The melody is not doubled by the piano, so special attention is required to keep the melodic intervals in tune. The opening interval for each verse is a leap up from low *so* to *mi*. Here students can practice approaching the higher pitch lightly from above, rather than straining for it from below.
Level of difficulty: Intermediate

Composer: Walters, Edmund
Title: Ding-Dong-Doh
Publisher: Boosey & Hawkes #5997
Voicing: Unison, piano accompaniment (optional orchestra; audience participation)
Style: Contemporary
Language: English
Notes: This is one of several carols composed for children's choirs from Liverpool, England, for their annual Christmas concerts. This song has two verses and a coda, and within each verse the structure of the melodic phrases is AA (in G major), BB (in E minor), and AA (in G major). Textural contrast is provided by an optional alto or descant part. The piano accompaniment is a reduction of the orchestral arrangement, which is available from the publisher.
Pedagogical value: The melodic intervals and rhythms are quite simple, making this song suitable for concentrating on shaping four-bar musical phrases. Using arc-shaped arm movements shows the shape of the phrase and encourages momentum. In addition, learning to go to the "ng" in the "ding-dong" will help to develop forward resonance.
Level of difficulty: Intermediate

Composer: Wessman, Harri
Title: Water Under Snow Is Weary (Vesi vasyy lumen alle)
Publisher: Walton Music Corp. WF-701
Voicing: Four parts, piano, flute, and optional string orchestra
Style: Contemporary
Language: English
Notes: Composed in triple meter (felt in one, conducted in three), this popular Finnish choral work for children's choir is accessible and easy to sing. Based on a haunting Finnish tune that is outlined by unison choir at the beginning of this composition, the chorus then divides into easily heard four-part diminished seventh chords. The piano plays repeated block chords in what approaches a swing style, while the flute plays an embellished version of the same tune heard at the beginning.
Pedagogical value: The singing of this work introduces young choirs to a unique style of choral singing. The work has a distinctly popular style, and the children enjoy the lilting triple meter and the snazzy-sounding seventh chords.
Level of difficulty: Intermediate

Composer: Wilder, Alec; arr. Donald P. Lang
Title: Lullabies and Nightsongs: Set I
Publisher: Boosey & Hawkes #6127
Voicing: Two parts, piano accompaniment
Style: Contemporary
Language: English
Notes: This is a delightful setting of four poems about the child's world of sleep and dreams. The titles are "Minnie and Winnie," "The Elephant Present," "The Star Lighter," and "The Answers." Each song is homophonic, with the melody in the soprano part. Though the tessitura of the alto part is low in the two-part section, there is ample unison singing to provide opportunities for both parts to use a wide vocal range. Contrast among the four songs is provided through the use of different meters and tonalities.
Pedagogical value: The rhythm in all four songs consists primarily of quarter, eighth, half, and dotted half notes—all familiar to young singers. In addition, there are no difficult melodic leaps; therefore, these songs are suitable for sight-reading.
Level of difficulty: Intermediate

Composer: Williamson, Warren, arr.

Title: Joshua Fit the Battle of Jericho

Publisher: Tetra/Continuo Music #TC 438

Voicing: Three parts, piano

Style: American folk (spiritual)

Language: English

Notes: The texture of this well-known spiritual changes frequently, providing interest and musical variety. The melody is assigned to the middle voice in the first two verses, while the outer voices provide rhythmically varied harmony. The third and fourth verses are arranged homophonically with the melody in the upper voice. The texture of the refrain changes after each: the refrain is sung in unison, then in two-part harmony with an ostinato pattern in the middle voice. The final refrain is a fuguelike section that builds toward a dramatic cadence. The piano accompaniment supports the harmonic structure and often uses a walking-bass pattern.

Pedagogical value: Young singers will be familiar with the melody and enjoy discovering the different compositional techniques used by the arranger. They will also have the opportunity to practice and perform correctly the syncopated rhythms so important in this style of music.

Level of difficulty: Advanced

Composer: Wilson, John F., arr.

Title: O Who's That Yonder?

Publisher: Hope Publishing #JW 7781

Voicing: Two parts, soloist, piano accompaniment

Style: American folk (plantation song)

Language: English

Notes: This song in AB form is based on an old plantation hymn. Though the B section is scored for men's and women's voices, the lower part can be sung by treble voices pitched an octave higher. The A section, in unison in Eb minor, contrasts with the B section, which is in harmony after a modulation to E minor. In the A section, a soloist is contrasted with the answering chorus, and in the B section the lower part echoes the upper (the text remains the same in both sections). This is a lovely, gentle song that is easily accessible.

Pedagogical value: Because the range is quite wide in this song, singers have the opportunity to learn to sing pitches at the lower end of their range—while using the same light tone quality with which they sing the higher pitches.

Level of difficulty: Beginning; for very young choirs

Composer: Wolf, Hugo
Title: Mausfallen Spruchlein (Mousetrap Saying)
Publisher: Boosey & Hawkes #6463
Voicing: Unison, piano accompaniment
Style: Romantic
Language: German/English
Notes: The text of this humorous song is an invitation from children to the mice to come out and play. As in most *lieder* from the Romantic period, there is an equality between the vocal line and the accompaniment, which, in this case, reflects the playful character of the text. The declamatory melodic line contains intervals that are logically placed within the harmonic structure of the phrases. The editor has provided a helpful phonetic pronunciation guide for the German text.
Pedagogical value: Students can observe how the melody reflects the words of the text in songs from the Romantic period. In addition, they become aware of the importance of articulation in communicating the expressiveness of the song.
Level of difficulty: Intermediate

Composer: Woodgate, Leslie, arr.
Title: Rocking
Publisher: Oxford University Press U15
Voicing: Unison, piano accompaniment
Style: Czechoslovakian folk (seasonal)
Language: English
Notes: The text in this edition is a translation by Percy Dearmer. The piece is in F major, in $\frac{2}{4}$ time, with a range from C_4 to D_5. It is strophic, in two verses with a very short piano introduction and interlude and a sung codetta (which echoes the last phrase). This is a charming setting of a fairly well known carol. It is out of print but available through Oxford's Choral Archives service; allow extra time for ordering.
Pedagogical value: This is an excellent song for very young choirs as they are challenged to maintain their head tone and tuning on the end of the first phrase, "sweetly sleep, do not stir," which is in close intervals (D, B♮, C). There are several opportunities for them to find slurred notes, and they enjoy working on the programmatic, heavy-light articulation of "we will *rock you*."
Level of difficulty: Beginning; for very young choirs

Composer: Work, John W., arr.

Title: Go Tell It on the Mountain

Publisher: Galaxy Music #1.1753.1

Voicing: Three parts, piano accompaniment

Style: American folk (spiritual)

Language: English

Notes: Most students will be familiar with the melody of this well-known spiritual, and this arrangement is quite accessible to young singers. The texture, which changes frequently, comprises unison, solo, and homophonic sections. The piano accompaniment varies with the vocal sections but frequently doubles the vocal parts.

Pedagogical value: This is one of the few good arrangements of spirituals for young singers and serves to provide young singers with an acquaintance with music of this style.

Level of difficulty: Intermediate

Composer: Yon, Pietro A.

Title: Gesu bambino (The Infant Jesus)

Publisher: J. Fischer & Bro. #FEC 4657

Voicing: Three parts, piano accompaniment

Style: Contemporary (seasonal)

Language: Latin/English

Notes: The solo-tutti setting of this beautiful carol features a solo that could be sung by either a student or an adult from the community. The tutti includes both three-part homophony and voices in unison. The form of this piece is ABAB with an ending coda. The shifting tonality from E major to G major adds harmonic interest to one of the most well loved Christmas carols.

Pedagogical value: The melodic rhythm of this piece in $\frac{12}{8}$ is characterized by a dotted eighth note followed by a sixteenth note. The challenge is to sing the phrases in a legato style while maintaining the precision of the dotted rhythms.

Level of difficulty: Intermediate

Composer: Zaninelli, Luigi

Title: Americana: Folk Song Suite

Publisher: Shawnee Press, Inc. #E-120

Voicing: Two parts, piano accompaniment

Style: American folk

Language: English

Notes: "Shenandoah," "Skip to My Lou," and "Sweet Betsy from Pike" provide the basis of this suite. The different musical settings, as well as changes in meter and tonality, provide variety and contrast. The altos have the melody in "Shenandoah" while the sopranos sing a descant. "Skip to My Lou" appears first in unison, next in a two-part homophonic setting, and finally in canon. The arrangement of "Sweet Betsy" gives both parts the opportunity to sing the melody. The young singers' familiarity with the folk tunes will serve as a motivating factor for learning this rather long piece.

Pedagogical value: Contrast in the musical character of each of the folk songs provides an opportunity to work on several vocal skills: long, legato phrasing in "Shenandoah," crisp articulation in "Skip to My Lou," and tuning of stepwise and larger intervals in "Sweet Betsy." In addition, there are a great many changes of tempo and dynamics necessary to a successful performance of this work.

Level of difficulty: Intermediate

Composer: Zaninelli, Luigi
Title: Eight Rounds for Children
Publisher: Walton Music Corp. #3400-1–3400-8
Voicing: Two-, three-, and four-part rounds; piano accompaniment
Style: Contemporary
Language: English

Notes: These eight rounds, all quite different, are wonderfully suited for young singers. The words are appealing, and the piano accompaniment is just right for the varied texts. Two quite different rounds, such as "Oh, See the Bird" (#3400-6), which is in triple meter and in a minor key, and "It's Not that Nina's Naughty" (#3400-8), in duple meter and a major key, should be programmed together. The remaining titles are "Up the Street the Band Is Marching Down" (#3400-1), "Poor Donna Dennis" (#3400-2), "A Child Who Is Bad" (#3400-3), "Winter Is Near" (#3400-4), "Pretty Perky Pia" (#3400-5), and "Peter Potter" (#3400-7).

Pedagogical value: Each round offers different musical concepts and styles to study and perform. Several of these pieces, such as "Peter Potter" and "Up the Street the Band Is Marching Down," require rhythmic singing. "The Child Who Is Bad" and "Oh, See the Bird" are to be sung in a legato style and thus should be approached through melodic shaping.
Level of difficulty: Beginning

Composer: Zaninelli, Luigi
Title: The Water Is Wide
Publisher: Shawnee Press #E-83
Voicing: Two parts, piano accompaniment
Style: American folk
Language: English

Notes: This beautiful folk song is arranged so that each of the three verses has a different setting: verse one is unison, verse two is homophonic, and verse three is set in strict imitative counterpoint. The piano accompaniment consists of a rolling arpeggiated figure, which is in contrast to the legato phrasing of the melody line.

Pedagogical value: The simple rhythm and predominantly stepwise motion of the melody makes this a good song for young singers to sight-read. Learning to sing through the whole notes will promote the smooth legato character of this song.
Level of difficulty: Intermediate

Index One: Composers or Arrangers

Note: This index contains listings for the arrangers as well as the composers of works for which that information is applicable. Annotations for these works are found under the names of the composers, which are listed here with the compositions' titles. Annotations for folk or traditional materials are found under the arrangers' names.

Glaser, Victoria	Schein: O Lovely Child (arr.)
Goetze, Mary	Ca' the Yowes (arr.); Crawdad Hole (arr.); Franck: Da pacem Domine (arr.); Dormi, Dormi (arr.); The Little Birch Tree (arr.); The Old Carrion Crow (arr.); Old Joe Clark (arr.); The Piglets' Christmas (arr.)
Grandi, Alesandro	Hodie, nobis de caelo
Grieg, Edvard	Three Songs
Grundman, Clare	Pat-A-Pan (arr.); Zoo Illogical
Hall, William	I Know Where I'm Goin' (arr.)
Handel, George Frideric	The Lord Is My Strength; O Let the Merry Bells Ring; O Lovely Peace, with Plenty Crown'd; Thanks Be to Thee; Where 'er You Walk
Hardwicke, Arthur	Old Man Noah
Hawkins, Walter	I'm Goin' Up a Yonder
Henderson, Ruth Watson	A la ferme; Fallis: Cinderella; Four Little Foxes; Tree Toad; You'll Never Guess What I Saw
Holst, Gustav von	The Corn Song
Hopson, Hal	Prayer for the Earth (arr.); Prayer of the Christmas Animals (arr.); Twelve Gates Into the City (arr.)
Howell, John Raymond	The Angel Gabriel
Hughes, Penelope	Christmas Time
Humperdinck, Engelbert	The Sandmen's Song and The Children's Prayer
Ives, Charles	A Christmas Carol
Jacob, Gordon	Brother James' Air
Jackson, Jill	Let There Be Peace on Earth
James, Will	Alleluia
Jenkyns, Peter	Bessie, The Black Cat; The Crocodile; Snakes
Jennings, Carolyn	Carol of the Cuckoo; Cat and Mouse
Jordanoff, Christine	Appalachian Suite (arr.)
Jothen, Michael	God Made Me!
Kabalevsky, Dmitry	Good Night
Kennedy, John Brodbin	Little Lamb, Who Made Thee

Kirkpatrick, Ralph	Away in a Manger
Klouse, Andrea	John Henry: The Real Story
Kodály, Zoltán	Ave Maria; Cease Your Bitter Weeping; Christmas Dance of the Shepherds; Ladybird; 'Mid the Oak Trees (arr.)
Kurth, Burton	A Cookie for Snip; Little Boy Blue; Robin's Breakfast
Lang, Donald P.	Wilder: Lullabies and Nightsongs: Set I (arr.)
Lassus, Orlande de	*See de Lassus, Rolande*
Lavater	Strauss: Tales from the Vienna Woods (arr.)
Leslie, Kenneth	Cape Breton Lullaby
Lotti, Antonio	Miserere Mei
Lübeck, Vincent	A Christmas Cantata
Luboff, Norman	A Capital Ship (arr.)
McAfee, Donald	Schütz: Create in Me a Clean Heart (arr.)
MacCillivray, Allister	Song for the Mira
McKelvy, James	Deck the Halls in $\frac{7}{8}$ (arr.)
Mahler, Gustav	Bell Chorus
Martens, Dennis	Vivaldi: Gloria in excelsis (arr.)
Martin, William	Charlottown
Mason, Lowell	O Music (arr.)
Mendelssohn, Felix	Ye Sons of Israel
Miller, Sy	Let There Be Peace on Earth
Mozart, Wolfgang Amadeus	Ave Verum Corpus
Nelson, Havelock	Stay, Little Blackbird
Nelson, Ron	Ask the Moon; Autumn Lullaby for the Moon; Four Anthems for Young Choirs; He Came Here for Me; Miniatures from a Bestiary, Part I; Miniatures from a Bestiary, Part II; The Moon Does Not Sleep; Slumber Now Beloved Child
Niles, John Jacob	I Wonder as I Wander
Nordoff, Paul	My Lord, What a Morning (arr.)
Orrego Salas, Juan	Canticos de Navidad
Ouchterlony, David	The Gentle Donkey; On the Night When Jesus Was Born

Page, Nick	Niska Banja (arr.)
Palestrina, G. P.	Gloria Patri
Parke, Dorothy	The Ferryman; Who's That a-Knocking?
Persichetti, Vincent	sam was a man
Peterson, Oscar	Hymn to Freedom
Pinkham, Daniel	Angels Are Everywhere; Ave Maria; Evergreen
Poston, Elizabeth	Dance to Your Daddie (arr.)
Praetorius, Michael	How Brightly Shines the Morning Star; Jubilate Deo; Lo, How a Rose E'er Blooming; Psallite
Proulx, Richard	Boyce: Alleluia Round (arr.)
Purcell, Henry	Shepherd, Shepherd, Leave Decoying; Sound the Trumpet
Raminsh, Imant	Daybreak Song; Song of the Stars; The Sower; The Sun Is a Luminous Shield
Rao, Doreen	Kabelevsky: Good Night (arr.); Hashivenu (arr.); Bach: How Brightly Shines the Morning Star (arr.); De Lassus: Musica Dei bonum optimi; Mason: O Music (arr.); Praetorius: How Brightly Shines the Morning Star (arr.); Schubert: To Music (arr.); Sweelink: Vanitas, vanitatum (arr.)
Richardson, Michael	A Hundred Pipers (arr.); Promised Land (arr.)
Rowley, Alec	Suo-Gan
Runyan, Michael	Pine Grove; Shade of Night; Wings of Morning
Rutter, John	Donkey Carol; For the Beauty of the Earth; Jesus Child; Nativity Carol; Shepherd's Pipe Carol
Saint-Saëns, Camille	Praise Ye the Lord
Salieri, Antonio	Chimes
Schein, Johann	Kikkehihi; O Lovely Child
Schubert, Franz	Fischerweise; Peace; Sanctus; To Music
Schultz, Donna G.	Orkney Lullaby
Schumann, Robert	Autumn Song; Were I a Tiny Bird
Schütz, Heinrich	Lord, Create in Me a Clean Heart
Shaw, Geoffrey	The Golden Vanity (arr.)

Woodgate, Leslie	Rocking (arr.)
Work, John W.	Go Tell It on the Mountain (arr.)
Yon, Pietro A.	Gesu bambino
Zaninelli, Luigi	Americana: Folk Song Suite; Eight Rounds for Children; The Water Is Wide

Index Two: Titles

Cat of Cats, The	Carto, Tom
Ca' the Yowes	Goetze, Mary
Cease Your Bitter Weeping	Kodály, Zoltán
Charlottown	Martin, William
Children's Christmas Song	Vaughan Williams, Ralph
The Children's Prayer	Humperdinck, Engelbert
A Child's Book of Beasts	Berger, Jean
Chimes	Sallieri, Antonio
Ching-a-ring Chaw	Copland, Aaron
The Christ Child	Binkerd, Gordon
A Christmas Cantata	Lübeck, Vincent
A Christmas Carol	Ives, Charles
Christmas Dance of the Shepherds	Kodály, Zoltán
Christmas Time	Hughes, Penelope
Cinderella	Fallis, Lois
Come Now and Gather	Track, Gerhardt
A Cookie for Snip	Kurth, Burton
The Corn Song	Holst, Gustav von
Crawdad Hole	Goetze, Mary
Create in Me a Clean Heart	Schütz, Heinrich
Cripple Creek	Crocker, Emily
Crocodile, The	Jenkyns, Peter
The Cuckoo Carol	Walters, Edmund
Cuckoo, The	Smith, Gregg
Da pacem Domine	Franck, Melchior
Dance to Your Daddie	Poston, Elizabeth
Dance with Me	Davidson, Charles
Daybreak Song	Raminsh, Imant
Dead in the Cold	Finzi, Gerald
Deck the Halls in $\frac{7}{8}$	McKelvy, James
Die Meere	Brahms, Johannes
Die Schwestern	Brahms, Johannes
Ding-Dong-Doh	Walters, Edmund
Domine Deus	Bach, Johann Sebastian
Donkey Carol	Rutter, John
Don't Ask Me!	Berkowitz, Sol
Don't Leave Me	Bartók, Belá
Dormi, Dormi	Goetze, Mary

I Know Where I'm Goin'	Hall, Willam
I Will Praise the Lord	Bach, Johann Sebastian
I Wonder as I Wander	Niles, John Jacob
Il Court, le furet	Biggs, John
In the Valley	Davidson, Charles
I'm Goin' Up a Yonder	Hawkins, Walter
Jesus Child	Rutter, John
John Henry: The Real Story	Klouse, Andrea
Joshua Fit the Battle of Jericho	Williamson, Warren
Jubilate Deo	Praetorius, Michael
Kikkehihi	Schein, Johann
Kitty of Coleraine	Thiman, Eric H.
Kookaburra	Curtright, Carolee
Ladybird	Kodály, Zoltán
Land of Our Birth	Vaughan Williams, Ralph
Laudamus Te	Vivaldi, Antonio
Laughing and Shouting for Joy	Bach, Johann Sebastian
Let There Be Peace on Earth	Miller, Sy & Jackson, Jill
Linden Lea	Vaughan Williams, Ralph
The Little Birch Tree	Goetze, Mary
Little Boy Blue	Kurth, Burton
The Little Drummer Boy	Simeone, Davis, and Onorati
The Little Horses	Copland, Aaron
Little Lamb, Who Made Thee	Kennedy, John Brodbin
Long Long Ago	Floyd, Carlisle
Lord, Create in Me a Clean Heart	Schutz, Heinrich
The Lord Is My Strength	Handel, George Frideric
Lord, See the Good Works of My Heart	Bach, Johann Sebastian
Lo, How a Rose E'er Blooming	Praetorius, Michael
Lullabies and Nightsongs	Wilder, Alec
Lullaby, O Lullaby	Finzi, Gerald
Margaret Has a Milking Pail	Finzi, Gerald
Marienwuermchen	Brahms, Johannes
Mausfallen Spruchlein	Wolf, Hugo
May Day Carol	Bertaux, Betty

Pick a Bale of Cotton	Bertaux, Betty
The Piglets' Christmas	Goetze, Mary
Pine Grove	Runyan, Michael
The Place of the Blest	Thompson, Randall
Praise Ye the Lord	Saint-Saëns, Camille
Prayer for the Earth	Hopson, Hal
Prayer of the Christmas Animals	Hopson, Hal
Promised Land	Richardson, Michael
Psallite	Praetorius, Michael
Rejoice and Be Glad	Track, Gerhardt
Rejoice, O My Spirit	Bach, Johann Sebastian
Robin's Breakfast	Kurth, Burton
Rocking	Felciano, Richard
Rocking	Woodgate, Leslie
The Sally Gardens	Britten, Benjamin
sam was a man	Persichetti, Vincent
Sanctus	Schubert, Franz
Saucy Sailor, The	Specht, Judy
Shade of Night	Runyan, Michael
The Shenandoah Blues	Elliott, David
Shepherd's Pipe Carol	Rutter, John
Shepherd, Shepherd, Leave Decoying	Purcell, Henry
She's Like the Swallow	Vaughan Williams, Ralph
Simple Gifts	Copland, Aaron
The Sleep of the Child Jesus	Gevaert, Francois
Slumber Now Beloved Child	Nelson, Ron
Snakes	Jenkyns, Peter
The Snow Lay on the Ground	Sowerby, Leo
Song for the Mira	MacCillivray, Allister
Song of Innocence	Binkerd, Gordon
Song of the Stars	Raminsh, Imant
Songs for Judith	Drynan, Margaret
Sound the Trumpet	Purcell, Henry
The Sower	Raminsh, Imant
Space Travellers	Stone, David
Spring	Vaughan Williams, Ralph
Stay, Little Blackbird	Nelson, Havelock

Index Three: Voicings

Unison

Howell, John Raymond	The Angel Gabriel
Hughes, Penelope	Christmas Time
Ives, Charles	A Christmas Carol
Jenkyns, Peter	Bessie, The Black Cat; The Crocodile; Snakes
Jennings, Carolyn	Carol of the Cuckoo
Jothen, Michael	God Made Me!
Kirkpatrick, Ralph	Away in a Manger
Kurth, Burton	A Cookie for Snip; Little Boy Blue; Robin's Breakfast
Mahler, Gustav	Bell Chorus
Mason, Lowell	O Music
Nelson, Havelock	Stay, Little Blackbird
Nelson, Ron	Four Anthems for Young Choirs; Miniatures from a Bestiary, Part I
Nordoff, Paul	My Lord, What a Morning
Ouchterlony, David	The Gentle Donkey; On the Night When Jesus Was Born
Parke, Dorothy	The Ferryman; Who's That a-Knocking?
Pinkham, Daniel	Evergreen
Praetorius, Michael	Jubilate Deo
Rao, Doreen	Hashivenu
Rowley, Alec	Suo-Gan
Rutter, John	Jesus Child; Nativity Carol; Shepherd's Pipe Carol
Schubert, Franz	Fischerweise; Peace; To Music
Shaw, Geoffrey	The Golden Vanity
Sleeth, Natalie	O Come, O Come Immanuel
Specht, Judy	The Saucy Sailor
Sprenkle, Elam	For a Dewdrop; October's Party
Stone, David	Space Travellers
Thiman, Eric H.	Kitty of Coleraine; The Path to the Moon

Vaughan Williams, Ralph	An Invitation; Land of Our Birth; Linden Lea; She's Like the Swallow; Spring; To the Ploughboy; Two Songs of Winter
Walters, Edmund	Ding-Dong-Doh
Wolf, Hugo	Mausfallen Spruchlein
Woodgate, Leslie	Rocking

Two-Part Treble

Bach, Johann Sebastian	Domine Deus; I Will Praise the Lord; Laughing and Shouting for Joy; Lord, See the Good Works of My Heart; We Hasten with Faltering Footsteps
Bacon, Ernst	Buttermilk Hill
Bartók, Belá	Breadbaking; Don't Leave Me
Berger, Jean	A Child's Book of Beasts
Binkerd, Gordon	The Christ Child
Bissell, Keith	When I Set Out for Lyonesse
Brahms, Johannes	Die Meere; Die Schwestern
Carto, Tom	The Cat of Cats
Chass, Blanche	Hanerot Halalu
Copland, Aaron	The Little Horses; Simple Gifts
Crocker, Emily	Cripple Creek
De Cormier, Robert	The Erie Canal
Dvorak, Antonin	The Dove and the Maple Tree; Flow, Danube, Ebb and Flow
Elliott, David	The Shenandoah Blues
Fauré, Gabriel	Messe basse
Felciano, Richard	Rocking
Finzi, Gerald	Dead in the Cold; Margaret Has a Milking Pail
Floyd, Carlisle	Long Long Ago
Gershwin, George	Strike Up the Band
Goetze, Mary	Ca' the Yowes; The Old Carrion Crow
Grandi, Alesandro	Hodie, nobis de caelo
Grieg, Edvard	Three Songs

153

Sibelius, Jean	For Thee, Suomi
Simeone, Davis, and Onorati	The Little Drummer Boy
Smith, Gregg	The Cuckoo
Starer, Robert	Midnight
Strauss, Johann	Tales from the Vienna Woods
Tallis, Thomas	The Tallis Canon
Thiman, Eric H.	I Have Twelve Oxen; When Cats Run Home
Thompson, Randall	Velvet Shoes
Thomson, Virgil	My Shepherd Will Supply My Need
Tidball, Norman	Boots and Saddles
Track, Gerhardt	Come Now and Gather; Rejoice and Be Glad
Vaughan Williams, Ralph	Children's Christmas Song
Vivaldi, Antonio	Laudamus Te
Walters, Edmund	The Cuckoo Carol
Wilder, Alec	Lullabies and Nightsongs
Wilson, John F.	O Who's That Yonder?
Zaninelli, Luigi	Americana: Folk Song Suite; The Water Is Wide

Three-Part Treble

Beethoven, Ludwig van	Abbé Stadler
Berger, Jean	Fin, Feather and Fur
Berkowitz, Sol	Don't Ask Me!; I Had a Little Pup
Bertaux, Betty	May Day Carol; Who Killed Cock Robin
Biggs, John	Il court, le furet
Binkerd, Gordon	Song of Innocence
Boyce, William	Alleluia Round
Britten, Benjamin	This Little Babe
Byrd, William	Non Nobis Domine
Carto, Tom	Muddy Puddle
Curtright, Carolee	Kookaburra

Runyan, Michael	Pine Grove; Shade of Night; Wings of Morning
Salas, Juan Orrego	Canticos de Navidad
Schein, Johann	Kikkehihi
Schubert, Franz	Sanctus
Sowerby, Leo	The Snow Lay on the Ground
Strommen, Carl	Dream Angus
Thompson, Randall	The Place of the Blest
Vaughan Williams, Ralph	Orpheus with His Lute
Vivaldi, Antonio	Gloria in excelsis
Williamson, Warren	Joshua Fit the Battle of Jericho
Work, John W.	Go Tell It on the Mountain
Yon, Pietro A.	Gesu bambino

Four-Part Treble

Bertaux, Betty	An Apple with Its Seeds; Pick a Bale of Cotton; S'vivon
Copland, Aaron	Ching-a-ring Chaw
De Lassus, Rolande	Musica Dei donum optimi
Franck, Melchior	Da pacem Domine
Hawkins, Walter	I'm Goin' Up a Yonder
Nelson, Ron	He Came Here for Me
Page, Nick	Niska Banja
Sweelinck, Jan Pieterszoon	Vanitas, vanitatum
Wessman, Harri	Water Under Snow Is Weary

Index Four: Level of Difficulty

For Beginning Choirs

Bach, Johann Sebastian	Gloria! The World Rejoices; How Brightly Shines the Morning Star; Rejoice, O My Spirit
Baynon, Arthur	Mrs. Jenny Wren
Bertaux, Betty	To Music; Who Killed Cock Robin
Boyce, William	Alleluia Round
Brahms, Johannes	Marienwuermchen
Britten, Benjamin	The New Year Carol; Old Abram Brown; Oliver Cromwell; The Sally Gardens
Broughton, Marilyn	My Caterpillar; Nursery Rhyme Nonsense
Chass, Blanche	Hanerot Halalu
Cockshott, Gerald	Three French Carols
Copland, Aaron	Simple Gifts
Crocker, Emily	Cripple Creek
Curtright, Carolee	Kookaburra
Davidson, Charles	In the Valley
De Cormier, Robert	The Erie Canal
Drynan, Margaret	Songs for Judith
Fallis, Lois	Cinderella
Felciano, Richard	Rocking
Finzi, Gerald	Lullaby, O Lullaby; Margaret Has a Milking Pail
Floyd, Carlisle	Two Stephenson Songs
Foster, Anthony	Two Tongue-Twisters
Franck, Melchior	Da pacem Domine

Goetze, Mary	Ca' the Yowes; Dormi, Dormi; The Little Birch Tree; The Old Carrion Crow; The Piglets' Christmas
Grundman, Clare	Pat-A-Pan; Zoo Illogical
Hall, William	I Know Where I'm Goin'
Handel, George Frideric	Thanks Be to Thee
Henderson, Ruth Watson	A la ferme; You'll Never Guess What I Saw
Hopson, Hal	Prayer for the Earth; Prayer of the Christmas Animals; Twelve Gates Into the City
Howell, John Raymond	The Angel Gabriel
Hughes, Penelope	Christmas Time
Jenkyns, Peter	Bessie, The Black Cat; The Crocodile; Snakes
Jennings, Carolyn	Carol of the Cuckoo; Cat and Mouse
Jothen, Michael	God Made Me
Kabalevsky, Dmitri	Good Night
Kennedy, John Brodbin	Little Lamb, Who Made Thee
Kirkpatrick, Ralph	Away in a Manger
Kurth, Burton	A Cookie for Snip; Little Boy Blue; Robin's Breakfast
Mahler, Gustav	Bell Chorus
Mason, Lowell	O Music
Nelson, Havelock	Stay, Little Blackbird
Nelson, Ron	Four Anthems for Young Choirs
Nordoff, Paul	My Lord, What a Morning
Ouchterlony, David	The Gentle Donkey; On the Night When Jesus Was Born
Parke, Dorothy	The Ferryman; Who's That a-Knocking?
Pinkham, Daniel	Evergreen
Praetorius, Michael	Jubilate Deo
Rao, Doreen	Hashivenu

159

For Intermediate Choirs

Brahms, Johannes	Die Meere; Die Schwestern
Britten, Benjamin	This Little Babe
Byrd, William	Non Nobis Domine
Carto, Tom	The Cat of Cats; Muddy Puddle
Copland, Aaron	The Little Horses
Davidson, Charles	Dance with Me
De Lassus, Rolande	Musica Dei donum optimi
Dvorak, Antonin	The Dove and the Maple Tree; Flow, Danube, Ebb and Flow
Elliott, David	The Shenandoah Blues
Fauré, Gabriel	Messe basse
Finzi, Gerald	Dead in the Cold
Fitzgerald, Ella	A-Tisket, A-Tasket
Floyd, Carlisle	Long Long Ago
Gabrieli, Andrea	Ave Maria
Gershwin, George	Strike Up the Band
Gevaert, François	The Sleep of the Child Jesus
Goetze, Mary	Crawdad Hole
Grandi, Alesandro	Hodie, nobis de caelo
Grieg, Edvard	Three Songs
Handel, George Frideric	The Lord Is My Strength; O let the Merry Bells Ring; O Lovely Peace, with Plenty Crown'd; Where 'er You Walk
Hardwicke, Arthur	Old Man Noah
Hawkins, Walter	I'm Goin' Up a Yonder
Henderson, Ruth Watson	Tree Toad
Holst, Gustav von	The Corn Song
Humperdinck, Engelbert	The Sandman's Song and The Children's Prayer
Ives, Charles	A Christmas Carol
Jacob, Gordon	Brother James' Air
James, Will	Alleluia

Shaw, Geoffrey	The Golden Vanity
Sibelius, Jean	For Thee, Suomi
Simeone, Davis, and Onorati	The Little Drummer Boy
Smith, Gregg	The Cuckoo
Sowerby, Leo	The Snow Lay on the Ground
Sprenkle, Elam	For a Dewdrop; October's Party
Strauss, Johann	Tales from the Vienna Woods
Strommen, Carl	Dream Angus
Sweelinck, Jan Pieterszoon	Vanitas, vanitatum
Thompson, Randall	Velvet Shoes; My Shepherd Will Supply My Need
Track, Gerhardt	Come Now and Gather; Rejoice and Be Glad
Vaughan Williams, Ralph	Children's Christmas Song; An Invitation; Land of Our Birth; Spring; To the Ploughboy; Two Songs of Winter
Walters, Edmund	The Cuckoo Carol; Ding-Dong-Doh
Wessman, Harri	Water Under Snow Is Weary
Wilder, Alec	Lullabies and Nightsongs
Wolf, Hugo	Mausfallen Spruchlein
Work, John W.	Go Tell It on the Mountain
Yon, Pietro A.	Gesu bambino
Zaninelli, Luigi	Americana: Folk Song Suite; The Water Is Wide

For Advanced Choirs

Bach, Johann Sebastian	Domine Deus; I Will Praise the Lord; Lord, See the Good Works of My Heart; We Hasten with Faltering Footsteps
Bartók, Belá	Breadbaking
Binkerd, Gordon	The Christ Child; Song of Innocence
Bissell, Keith	When I Set Out for Lyonesse
Copland, Aaron	Ching-a-ring Chaw

For Very Young Choirs (K–3)

Brahms, Johannes	Marienwuerchen
Britten, Benjamin	The New Year Carol; Old Abram Brown; Oliver Cromwell; The Sally Gardens
Broughton, Marilyn	My Caterpillar; Nursery Rhyme Nonsense
Cockshott, Gerald	Three French Carols
Davidson, Charles	In the Valley
De Cormier, Robert	The Erie Canal
Drynan, Margaret	Songs for Judith
Fallis, Lois	Cinderella
Felciano, Richard	Rocking
Finzi, Gerald	Lullaby, O Lullaby
Floyd, Carlisle	Two Stephenson Songs
Foster, Anthony	Two Tongue-Twisters
Franck, Melchior	Da paccm Domine
Goetze, Mary	Dormi, Dormi; The Little Birch Tree; The Piglets' Christmas
Grundman, Clare	Pat-A-Pan; Zoo Illogical
Hall, William	I Know Where I'm Goin'
Hopson, Hal	Prayer for the Earth; Prayer of the Christmas Animals; Twelve Gates Into the City;
Howell, John Raymond	The Angel Gabriel
Jenkyns, Peter	Bessie, The Black Cat; The Crocodile; Snakes
Jennings, Carolyn	Carol of the Cuckoo; Cat and Mouse
Kabalevsky, Dmitri	Good Night
Kennedy, John Brodbin	Little Lamb, Who Made Thee
Kirkpatrick, Ralph	Away in a Manger
Kurth, Burton	A Cookie for Snip; Little Boy Blue; Robin's Breakfast
Mason, Lowell	O Music
Nelson, Havelock	Stay, Little Blackbird

1502-10-2M-3/90